# Regional Disorder:
# The South China Sea Disputes

Sarah Raine and Christian Le Mière

# Regional Disorder:
# The South China Sea Disputes

Sarah Raine and Christian Le Mière

 IISS The International Institute for Strategic Studies

# The International Institute for Strategic Studies

Arundel House | 13–15 Arundel Street | Temple Place | London | WC2R 3DX | UK

First published March 2013 by **Routledge**
4 Park Square, Milton Park, Abingdon, Oxon, OX14 4RN

for **The International Institute for Strategic Studies**
Arundel House, 13–15 Arundel Street, Temple Place, London, WC2R 3DX, UK
www.iiss.org

Simultaneously published in the USA and Canada by **Routledge**
270 Madison Ave., New York, NY 10016

*Routledge is an imprint of Taylor & Francis, an Informa Business*

© 2013 The International Institute for Strategic Studies

DIRECTOR-GENERAL AND CHIEF EXECUTIVE Dr John Chipman
EDITOR Dr Nicholas Redman
ASSISTANT EDITOR Nadine El-Hadi
EDITORIAL Nicholas Payne, Jeffrey Mazo
COVER/PRODUCTION John Buck, Kelly Verity
COVER IMAGE iStockphoto.com/Yuri Arcurs

**The International Institute for Strategic Studies** is an independent centre for research, information and debate on the problems of conflict, however caused, that have, or potentially have, an important military content. The Council and Staff of the Institute are international and its membership is drawn from almost 100 countries. The Institute is independent and it alone decides what activities to conduct. It owes no allegiance to any government, any group of governments or any political or other organisation. The IISS stresses rigorous research with a forward-looking policy orientation and places particular emphasis on bringing new perspectives to the strategic debate.

The Institute's publications are designed to meet the needs of a wider audience than its own membership and are available on subscription, by mail order and in good bookshops. Further details at www.iiss.org.

Printed and bound in Great Britain by Bell & Bain Ltd, Thornliebank, Glasgow

British Library Cataloguing in Publication Data
A catalogue record for this book is available from the British Library

Library of Congress Cataloging in Publication Data

ADELPHI series
ISSN 1944-5571

ADELPHI 436–437
ISBN 978-0-415-70262-1

# Contents

Map 1: **Potential and claimed maritime zones in the South China Sea**

| Km | 100 | 200 | 300 |
| Miles | 50 | 100 | 150 | 200 |

Shading = 200nm exclusive economic zone claims based on coastlines (including Pratas Island but excluding Paracel Islands). China/Taiwan EEZ shown as one claim.

Possible exclusive economic zones generated by Paracel and Spratly Islands, assuming island status for small number of features deemed able to qualify under UNCLOS and equidistance with overlapping EEZs.

China's 'nine-dashed line'

Philippine Kalayaan Island Group limits (declared 1978)

CHINA

Pratas Island

Hainan

Yalong Bay

Common Fishery Zone

Paracel Islands

Macclesfield Bank

PHILIPPINES

Scarborough Reef

Subic Bay

VIETNAM

SOUTH

CHINA

Mindoro Strait

Cam Ranh Bay

SEA

Spratly Islands

MALAYSIA

BRUNEI

INDONESIA

INDONESIA

Sources: The Philippine Inquirer; The New York Times; BBC News; Google Earth; Thao, Nguyen Hong, Maritime Delimitation and Fishery Cooperation in the Tonkin Gulf (Ocean Development and International Law 2005); UNCLOS; Maritime Briefing Volume 1 Number 6 (International Boundaries Research Unit, 1995); Mark J. Valencia, Jon M. Van Dyke, and Noel A. Ludwig, Sharing the Resources of the South China Sea (Honolulu: University of Hawaii Press, 1999); US Energy Information Administration (EIA).

Map 2: **Hydrocarbon concessions and proven reserves in the South China Sea**

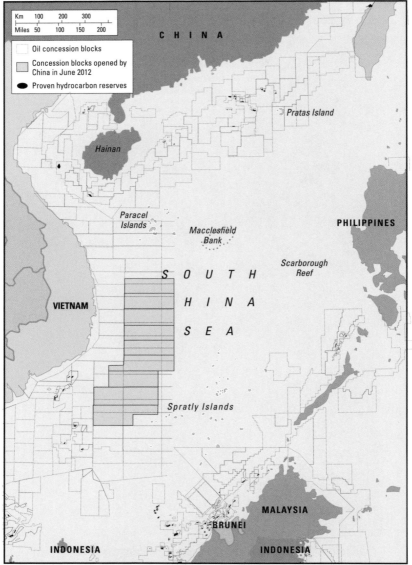

Sources: Office of the Geographer, US Department of State, 803425AI (G02257) 1-10. This map can be found on the National University of Singapore's website, at: http://cil.nus.edu.sg/wp/wp-content/uploads/2011/06/75967_South-China-Sea-1.pdf; Vietnamese Embassy, London.
Hydrocarbon reserves are proven or actively being exploited. Estimates of possible/probable reserves vary widely.

Map 3: **Occupations of the Spratly and Paracel Islands**

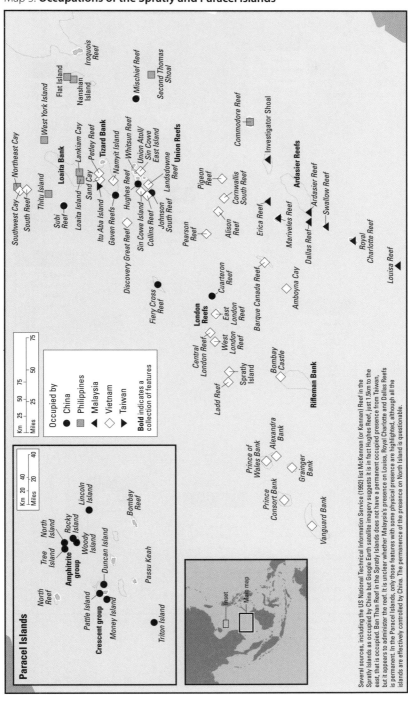

Several sources, including the US National Technical Information Service (1992) list McKennan (or Kennan) Reef in the Spratly Islands as occupied by China but Google Earth satellite imagery suggests it is in fact Hughes Reef, just 1.5km to the east, that is occupied. Ban Than Reef in the Spratly Islands does not have a permanent occupied presence from Taiwan, but it appears to administer the reef. It is unclear whether Malaysia's presence on Louisa, Royal Charlotte and Dallas Reefs is permanent. In the Paracel Islands, only those features with some physical presence are highlighted, although all the islands are effectively controlled by China. The permanence of the presence on North Island is questionable.

Source: The IISS, Google Earth.

Map 4: **Naval and maritime paramilitary capabilities**

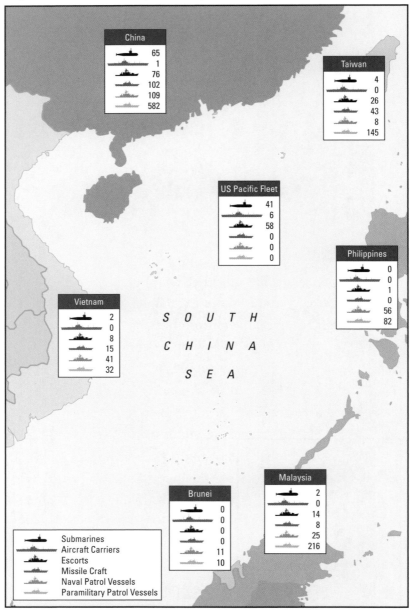

**China**
- 65
- 1
- 76
- 102
- 109
- 582

**Taiwan**
- 4
- 0
- 26
- 43
- 8
- 145

**US Pacific Fleet**
- 41
- 6
- 58
- 0
- 0
- 0

**Philippines**
- 0
- 0
- 1
- 0
- 56
- 82

**Vietnam**
- 2
- 0
- 8
- 15
- 41
- 32

**Malaysia**
- 2
- 0
- 14
- 8
- 25
- 216

**Brunei**
- 0
- 0
- 0
- 0
- 11
- 10

*S O U T H*

*C H I N A*

*S E A*

Legend:
- Submarines
- Aircraft Carriers
- Escorts
- Missile Craft
- Naval Patrol Vessels
- Paramilitary Patrol Vessels

Capabilities for China include all three fleets of the People's Liberation Army Navy, and hence may not be based in the South China Sea. Capabilites for the US Pacific Fleet are based in Japan, Guam, Hawaii and west coast contiguous United States.
Source: *The Military Balance 2013*

# INTRODUCTION

Asia is in transition like no other continent on Earth. Home to China (perceived as the next challenger to American hegemony) and rising powers from India to Indonesia, it hosts some of the world's fastest-growing economies, as well as its largest population of young people, with almost two out of every three people between 15–24 years of age living in Asia.[1] Furthermore, this continent has the greatest numbers of men under arms and an increasing share of the world's defence spending. As the global balance of power shifts eastwards, so too does the centre of gravity of the world's security and prosperity challenges.[2] And at the heart of this new centre in the east is the sea.

The influence of sea power on history has long been studied, not least by the nineteenth-century naval professor and geostrategist Alfred Thayer Mahan, who emphasised the importance of sea power on the long-term success of a country's international relations.[3] More recently, maritime history professor Geoffrey Till has suggested four key and interdependent attributes of sea power: the sea as a medium for trade; the sea as a resource, in terms of what lies within, as well as underneath, its waters;

the sea as a medium for informational and cultural exchange; and finally, but perhaps most importantly, the sea as a medium for dominion.[4] The South China Sea, which lies at the nexus of Southeast and Northeast Asia – at the meeting point of global sea routes – and offers the shortest route between the Indian and the Western Pacific Oceans, exemplifies all of these attributes.

This sea carries more than half of the world's annual merchant-fleet tonnage and a third of all maritime traffic.[5] A growing dynamic of intra-regional as well as inter-regional trade ensures a regular flow of raw materials and commodities across its waters, enveloping both Southeast and Northeast Asia in concerns over sea lines of communications (SLOCs) within these waters. In total, around US$5.3trillion in trade flows through the region around the South China Sea each year, with one-fifth of this being US commerce.[6] A vital part of this maritime traffic is the passage of hydrocarbons to a resource-hungry east. Around 80% of China's crude-oil imports, about 66% of South Korea's energy supplies and nearly 60% of Japan's and Taiwan's arrive via this sea.[7] Whilst the Middle East continues to be the main supplier of these resources, an increasing percentage is also arriving from Africa, thereby further expanding the web of parties with a stake in maritime security in the South China Sea.

Rapid industrialisation, changing dietary requirements (in the form of increased demand for fish), and impressive year-on-year growth rates have all played their part in boosting maritime trade and merchant shipping within the region. There has been growing demand for dry-bulk goods, such as grains, as well as for break-bulk goods, such as iron ore for construction. Some of the world's biggest and busiest container ports, from Singapore to Hong Kong, are located around this sea, as several countries in the region have emerged as leading maritime nations with growing merchant fleets and world class ports.[8]

Within the South China Sea lie hundreds of small islands, atolls, rocks and reefs, only a small proportion of which are above water at high tide and which collectively form the focus for an intricate series of overlapping sovereignty disputes.[9] Indeed, even the different names used within the region for the sea itself, and the respective features therein, offer a repeated reminder of the complexity of these disputes. Although, for practical reasons, only the internationally recognised terminology for the South China Sea and its islands and groupings are used in this book, disagreements on these terminologies should at least be noted. For example, the South China Sea is known in China as the South Sea, but in Vietnam as the East Sea and in the Philippines as the West Philippine Sea.

### Disputes and disagreements: from regional to global

Amongst this plethora of features scattered throughout the sea are four island groupings claimed, to varying extents, by six separate claimants as follows:

- the Paracel Islands in the northwest, occupied by China, but claimed by Vietnam and Taiwan;
- the Pratas Islands in the northeast, occupied by Taiwan, but claimed by China;
- the Spratly Islands in the southeast, occupied in part by China, Taiwan, Vietnam, Malaysia and the Philippines, but claimed in their entirety by China, Taiwan and Vietnam and in part by Malaysia, the Philippines and Brunei;
- Macclesfield Bank/Scarborough Reef in the central and east-central sea, unoccupied, but both Macclesfield Bank and Scarborough Reef are claimed by China and Taiwan, whilst Scarborough Reef is also claimed by the Philippines.

As the next chapter explains, these claims – where they are clarified and expounded – are often grounded in a confusing, inconsistent, yet ruthlessly pragmatic mixture of international law and historic rights.

Alongside these overlapping territorial disputes concerning small patches of land runs a related dispute over the maritime boundaries generated by these assorted features under the 1982 United Nations Convention on the Law of the Sea (UNCLOS).[10] The intersecting nature of claims to sovereignty over land in the South China Sea have inevitably given rise to substantive conflicts also over maritime claims to Exclusive Economic Zones (EEZs). Under UNCLOS, different features generate dramatically different maritime zones, depending on whether they are defined as islands or something less substantial, such as rocks or low-tide elevations. Yet the precise classifications of the multitude of features sprawling across this sea are yet to be determined. Moreover, the prescription of maritime boundaries is further complicated by disputes over the drawing of baselines from which these maritime zones are then measured. This is ordinarily done from the low-water line along the coast, but, under UNCLOS, states can apply straight baselines where the coast is deeply indented or has a fringe of islands. They can also make applications for the recognition of an extended continental shelf, which then expands a state's resource rights from the standard 200 nautical miles from its baseline for sea and subsoil rights to up to 350 nautical miles from its baseline for subsoil rights alone. These straight baselines, as well as applications for extended continental shelves, are the subject of further contestation and controversy.

Finally, separate from the dispute between the six claimants on territorial sovereignty and maritime rights comes the debate – fronted by the US and China in the context of the South China Sea, but of relevance to a far broader audience – on what activities are permitted by one nation under the 'freedom of navigation' guarantee of UNCLOS within the EEZ of another nation. In particular, the focus is on what military activities, if any, can legally be carried out by one nation within the EEZ of another. The US has led the way in arguing that UNCLOS Article 58 allows states to enjoy unqualified freedom of navigation and overflight within an EEZ, including the right to conduct military activities such as surveillance and reconnaissance. China's interpretation, however, seems to be less liberal. It argues that such military activities are precluded without prior permission from the state to which the EEZ belongs, pointing to UNCLOS's requirement for 'due regard' to be paid to the rights of the state to whom the EEZ belongs.[11] So when, in March 2009, China responded forcefully to the USNS *Impeccable*'s trawling of an acoustic device, known as a towed-array sonar, within China's EEZ, it became the public face of a longer-running dispute over what was, or was not, legal activity within an EEZ. At least from China's perspective, the freedom to spy from the sea within another country's EEZ is not enshrined in international maritime law.

This *Impeccable* incident (explained in more detail in the next chapter) marked something of a turning point in the attention paid to the evolving security dynamics of the South China Sea in general, and to its sovereignty disputes in particular. Prior to this incident, in recent years the subject had been more the domain of the dedicated regional specialist than the global security generalist. Although rival claims over the disputed islands had escalated into armed conflict and spilt blood in the past, much of the decade prior to the *Impeccable* incident had been largely characterised by stagnation in terms of dispute prosecution. Indeed, the last significant military clash in the South China Sea took place in 1988, between Chinese and Vietnamese naval forces at Johnson Reef. But following the launch of China's charm offensive in Southeast Asia – which really began to pay dividends with China's 1997 decision not to devalue the yuan during the Asian financial crisis – regional dynamics improved remarkably. The signing in 2002 of a Declaration of Conduct in the South China Sea (DoC) between China and the Association of Southeast Asian Nations (ASEAN), aimed at the responsible management of conflicting sovereignty disputes within the sea, reflected as much as dictated these more positive dynamics. And whilst it may soon have become clear that the DoC was failing to deliver and that the rhetoric of cooperation did not match the reality of competition, these disputes still continued to attract relatively little attention from beyond the immediate region. Wars in Afghanistan and Iraq helped ensure that the focus of international attention lay elsewhere. When Southeast Asian officials murmured quietly, but repeatedly, to their Western counterparts about their concerns over the consequences of the perceived neglect of the region, the South China Sea was never far from their thoughts.

Yet as the decade wore on, the rapid progress of China's military modernisation became more apparent whilst the ultimate intentions behind the development of these capabilities became no less opaque. Longer-standing concerns over the impact of China's rise on the balance of power and regional order in East and Southeast Asia were brought more sharply into focus, both in the region and beyond. One reflection of these underlying concerns, and a factor that this book will go on to explore in more detail, has been the increasing militarisation of the South China Sea. For example, since the mid-2000s, China has built a major naval base on Hainan Island that is also likely to serve as a base, or at least key logistics node, for its future aircraft carrier(s) and as host for its most modern nuclear-powered attack and ballistic-missile submarines. Meanwhile, the harassment of US military vessels and US energy companies operating within the sea also helped ensure the return of the disputes to the global stage. And whilst economic indicators reveal a more integrated region than ever before, there has been a noticeable failure in the development of any parallel and similarly paced improvement in security relations. Indeed, if anything, the economic exposure of smaller and medium-sized powers in the region to the might of Chinese markets has only served to exacerbate feelings of insecurity about relations with their giant cousin.

## Beijing sets the tone

With 14 neighbours on land, eight at sea and the forward-deployed presence of the US to negotiate, China's regional environment is nothing if not complex. Meanwhile, with approximately half of China's total shoreline running adjacent to the South China Sea, the political, military, economic and resource interests of both Beijing and its relevant coastal provinces in this sea are both logical and well founded. For its part, China has long protested that its economic rise need not be accompanied by a parallel impact on the political order. It has, observers are repeatedly told, no hegemonic ambitions. Nevertheless, as China's economic interests have expanded so, inevitably, have its national interests and its global reach. Within the region, China is simply becoming too much of a presence not to be having an impact on the evolving political and security order. With its increased influence, Beijing appears to have grown more confident in both its ability and desire to be the protector of its own security interests. As President Hu Jintao opened the 18th Party Congress in November 2012, he argued for China's development 'into a maritime power', which would be 'resolute' in its safeguarding of China's maritime rights and interests.[12]

It is, therefore, to China that this book deliberately first turns in analysing the management the South China Sea disputes and their impact on the emerging regional order. It does so with the argument that, as the militarily and economically most capable of the claimant powers, Beijing bears something of a burden of responsibility in setting the tone and nature of dispute management in the South China Sea, and so, also, the balance between cooperation and competition in the region more generally.

Yet there are other dynamics at work in the South China Sea beyond the complicated geography of China's rise. In more general terms, the impact of globalisation and the shift in the relative balance of power that is resulting from the region's changing geoeconomics, coupled with the insecurity these changes are causing, would, in any case, be helping to force these disputes on to the international agenda.

Perhaps understandably, Beijing has little desire to see the South China Sea disputes take geopolitical centre-stage. Its diverse interests are better met through a quieter regional programme of bilateral diplomacy. So, while the US Quadrennial Defence Review of February 2010 reminded readers of US national-security interests in freedom of navigation within the global commons, referring to this sea as the 'connective tissue of the international system',[13] and Indian Foreign Minister S.M. Krishna cited the particular strategic and economic significance of the South China Sea as rendering it 'the property of the world', China has steadfastly objected to the attentions of 'outside' powers.[14] As one commentary in the Communist Party's *Global Times* responded to Krishna's comments: 'other countries can't denote one country's territory as global property'.[15] Yet Beijing's conservative attempts to push back against the realities of today's international interests and strategic concerns in the South China Sea are proving at best unproductive and, ultimately, as this book argues, even counterproductive. Whether Beijing likes it or not, the challenges posed by the management of security issues in the South China Sea have, to take a Chinese phrase, 'gone global'.[16]

## Southeast Asian states matter too

Yet as these disputes have gone global, so too often have Southeast Asian nations found themselves treated as the field for this new-found geopolitical competition surrounding the South China Sea, rather than players in their own right, with the capabilities and policies to impact actively on the evolution of these concerns. This is perhaps in part because a lot of the recent literature on the South China Sea has been in the form of op-eds, or perhaps only paper length. Meanwhile, more detailed studies concerned with the strategic implications of the South China Sea disputes have tended to approach the question from a US perspective – considering what US interests are at stake and what US policies should be followed.[17] This book is aimed, in part, at addressing this gap.

Despite the limitations of ASEAN (from which this book does not shy away), Southeast Asian nations have the potential to be, and in some cases already are, active catalysts, rather than passive recipients, of US–China security dynamics in the crucible of the South China Sea. They are the ones who will need to find imaginative ways to hold the door open for US security engagement in the region whilst they simultaneously look to strengthen their economic engagement with China and to hedge against a possible diminution of US influence in Asia with a cautious and, for the moment, largely symbolic security dialogue of their own with China.

Meanwhile, the ability of the region to develop its own effective regional security architecture and to manage the disputes in the South China Sea will be closely interlinked for some time to come. Success in one will feed into, and play off, success in the other. Alternatively, failure in one will have ominous consequences for the other. At present, Southeast Asia has a host of overlapping regional security organisations and, at least in theory therefore, a host of forums in which to discuss the South China Sea disputes. There is, for example, the broad-based membership of the ASEAN Regional Forum, which has traditionally taken the lead on maritime security issues. There is also the slightly more selective 18–member East Asia Summit (EAS), where the US in particular has been pushing for greater discussion of the South China Sea. Then there is ASEAN itself, which has traditionally been somewhat more hesitant in risking debate, and therefore disagreement, on the question of the disputes. Whilst some iterations of some of these institutions have been making some progress in taking a more active role in dispute management in recent years, as this book makes clear, their record to date is modest at best.

However, the advantages for the region in finding a way to lead in the brokering of these disputes, as opposed to simply following the dynamics set by others, are clear. Ultimately the smaller and medium-sized powers of Southeast Asia have a great deal to lose from a breakdown in US–China relations that would force them to choose between a US-centric model and a China-centric model for the region. Interestingly though, such countries could also fear losing out from a US–China condominium, which, in a G2 world in Asia at least, would carve out respective spheres of influence with minimal input from the smaller and medium-sized powers affected. Such a deal would likely involve tacit acknowledgement of the South China Sea as China's sphere of influence in return for Chinese restraint leading into the Western Pacific. As this book will go on to explore, managing the balance between these two polar alternatives can occasionally lead to elements of schizophrenia in Southeast Asian approaches to third-party engagement in the South China Sea.

## The US as monitor and arbiter

Naturally, as a 'resident power' in the Asia-Pacific, the US has also been paying close attention to these disputes.[18] Yet, its strategic room for manoeuvre in the South China Sea flows to a large extent from the landscape as defined by both China and Southeast Asia. The US needs close and cooperative partners in Southeast Asia, who remain supportive and interested in sustaining the US's leading role in the region and who stand ready to do more where necessary and possible, in particular in the light of obvious US budgetary constraints. Local attitudes to such requirements will inevitably evolve, informed, at least in part, by Chinese actions and activities in the region. US diplomacy will need to recognise that Washington's role as the primary provider of maritime public security goods in the region needs Southeast Asian approval, and so diplomacy will need to work hard at shaping and managing, with subtlety, perceptions that Southeast Asian states 'need' US support. Meanwhile, as frustrating as the US might find ongoing questioning of its long-term commitment to the region in the face of repeated rhetorical assurances to this effect, it will have to show consistency in matching actions with words. It should, for example, continue to 'show up' even as and when the agenda looks light on substance, settling for influence through engagement rather than through calculated distance.

The South China Sea will have a central role to play in the three-way probing of intent and ambition between China, the US and Southeast Asia within the context of an emerging regional order. Yet the stage management for dispute handling is becoming more rather than less complicated. There are simply more messages to send. The US, for its part, seeks to reassure China that it's Asia 'pivot' is not all about China, and that its re-energised engagement in the region is fully compatible with the rise of China. Alongside this, it seeks to remind

China that its actions in the South China Sea remain under scrutiny and that its rise cannot come at the expense of the US position in the region. Meanwhile, the US looks to reassure partners in Southeast Asia that it remains a reliable partner, committed for the long term. But it also has to guard against any danger that US partners in the region – for example its treaty ally, the Philippines – could feel emboldened by US support to the point that they would countenance a reckless and unnecessary provocation.

## Prospects and implications

As agendas surrounding the South China Sea become more crowded, so the prospects for dispute resolution continue to look bleak. The problems are too complex; the stakes are too high. There are too many overlapping claims by too many rival claimants of too many small maritime features, all within a sea that is host to useful reserves of untapped resources and is understood to be of particular geopolitical significance.

Although there are neutral forums to which mutually consenting parties can take their territorial and maritime disputes, the geopolitical implications of these disputes make international legal processes unlikely to be their ultimate determinant. It is, in practice, improbable that claimants will mutually agree to pass off decisions of such perceived significance to external arbitration. The attempt by the Philippines in January 2013 to refer China to an arbitral tribunal over the status of Scarborough Reef seems doomed to fail in legal terms (if not, importantly, in diplomatic terms too) as, when China ratified UNCLOS, it chose to opt out of Article 298 which provides for compulsory dispute settlement under the treaty.[19] In this regard, China's actions are no more 'assertive' than others, including Russia, France, Canada and South Korea, who have chosen to do likewise. Indeed, should the

US ever follow suit with its own ratification of UNCLOS, it is highly likely that it too would take the same opt-out. Whilst the key legal aspects of these disputes are therefore explained in the next chapter and expounded further in Appendix 1, this book is deliberately not a legal treatise, focused on what *should* be the case in the South China Sea, but rather a political examination of what *is* going on and what the implications of these activities and tensions could be. Due respect is therefore paid to the fundamental centrality of international law in dispute management and resolution, but recognition is also given to the broader realities of the geopolitical and geoeconomic context within which this dispute management is situated.

Indeed, with little prospect of an ultimate resolution in sight, it looks likely that the process of dispute management will matter almost as much as the eventual outcome. How China handles these disputes with its militarily and economically more vulnerable neighbours will offer potential clues as to what sort of regional power it is intent on becoming. For example, some have argued that the South China Sea will become for China in the twenty-first century what the Greater Caribbean was for an emerging US in the late nineteenth/early twentieth century. In other words, ascendancy in the South China Sea could become the key for eventual Chinese dominance within the Eastern Hemisphere in a way that American ascendancy in the Caribbean Basin provided the foothold for turn-of-the-century American dominance over the Western Hemisphere. As Chinese military modernisation advances, and the People's Liberation Army Navy (PLAN) in particular is seen as preparing to challenge the status quo in maritime Asia, how will China handle the understandable concern this is causing in the region and beyond? And how will ASEAN states respond? Can they confound the sceptics and muster sufficient unity to become an influential regional security organisation for this issue, despite the differences between the four claimants as well as between these four and the remaining six non-claimants? Or will ASEAN's efforts be insufficient to persuade an ever more powerful China to choose to behave with gallant restraint?

Although there are those who have offered a more optimistic assessment of how a less Westphalian, less state-centric, twenty-first-century political model might work to dampen the strategic value attached to the South China Sea, the concern remains that too many trends are pointing in the direction of further instability.[20] There will be more pressure on increasingly-scarce fishing resources and more pressure to claim precious hydrocarbons lying under the regional sea. Even during a global economic downturn, the strategic importance of seaborne trade and in particular of imported energy resources has not faded. Meanwhile, paramilitaries are expanding but the writing of rules of engagement and the setting of mechanisms for their control by the central authorities aren't always keeping up. Incidents at sea, between fishermen and fishery enforcement vessels, and, more worryingly, between rival paramilitaries and militaries are already too common and look set only to increase.

Talk of a 'strategic window of opportunity' is therefore beginning to abound. In Southeast Asia, this window of opportunity refers to restraining China whilst the US is still engaged in the region and before the relative balance of power has swung too far in China's favour. In China, this window of opportunity refers to a time when China has economic leverage and a competent military in reserve, but before unfavourable domestic economic indicators, such as its ageing population or fragilities in its significant shadow banking sector, might begin to sap away at this advantage.

## The South China Sea and the regional disorder

After a decade of relative neglect by all but a handful of regional security experts, the disputes in the South China Sea are once again, rightly, attracting the attention of the global security community. This book aims to offer an overview and analysis of the key issues to that interested but non-specialist community, casting these disputes within the broader context of the strategic competition that is unfolding in Southeast Asia and offering a substantive examination of the role of Southeast Asian nations themselves. It also hopes to engage the specialist community – who have long appreciated the strategic importance of the South China Sea but who have watched the waves of tension and resulting attention come and go before – on why this time might be different. The trends are worrying, the stakes are higher, and boundaries are being tested and defined, both literally and figuratively. The moves being made now matter for the precedents they are setting and the learning experiences they are providing. The canvas is not just regional, but global. If the Obama administration was to wish to find a 'pivot' within its rebalance to Asia, it needs look no further than the South China Sea.[21]

In considering this global backdrop, some have gone so far as to label the South China Sea as the 'future of conflict' in the twenty-first century; others meanwhile have argued that the flurry of media attention that this sea has commanded is disproportionate to the strategic challenge these disputes actually pose.[22] Although the authors of this book would not rule out escalation from individual incident to diplomatic and military crisis by accident rather than design, they have not spent their time researching and writing on this topic because they believe that large-scale bloodshed in the South China Sea is imminent. Indeed one point of intellectual curiosity for the South China Sea disputes is precisely that the challenges are more subtle than this.

Ultimately, the story of overlapping sovereignty disputes in the South China Sea is more than the story of who owns which islands. It is about how these disputes are managed, and in due course resolved. Will fundamental norms of international law and international relations prevail or will the increasing reserves of Chinese military and economic prowess prove more relevant? Might China's challenge to existing maritime norms, and in particular its interpretation of the implications of the Law of the Sea for the prohibition of foreign military activities in EEZs, begin to create a 'hairline fracture' in the legal framework and/or global order?[23]

The story of the South China Sea is also about domestic political will to manage rising popular nationalism and about international political will to find peaceful paths to inclusive security structures in Asia, with room for both the rising and the risen. And, perhaps most interestingly, it is about the impact of these shifting sands on the plethora of small and medium-sized actors in Southeast Asia and the emerging regional order that is being shaped therein. The story affects claimants and non-claimants, regional powers and extra-regional powers. It involves state actors, from capitals to their provinces, and it involves non-state actors including fishermen, oil companies, and even pirates.

The disputes that surround the South China Sea matter, then, not because they may yet prove to be a game changer in Asia – although they might. They matter because they are themselves reflective of the changing game in Asia.

# Notes

1  According to UN figures, 62% of the world's 15–24-year-olds live in Asia. Saira Syed, 'As Asia Booms, what is Cost of Success for its Young', *BBC News*, 7 November 2011, http://www.bbc.co.uk/news/business-15532821.

2  Kishore Mahbubahni may label this shift to an Asian hemisphere as 'irresistible' but there are plenty of domestic challenges and regional distrust which could yet seriously unseat this perceived momentum. Kishore Mahbubani, *The New Asian Hemisphere: The Irresistible Shift of Global Power to the East* (New York: Public Affairs, 2008).

3  Alfred Mahan, *The Influence of Seapower on History, 1660–1783* (Cambridge: Cambridge University Press, 2010).

4  Geoffrey Till, *Seapower: A Guide for the Twenty-First Century* (Oxford: Taylor and Francis, 2009).

5  Robert Kaplan, 'The Vietnam Solution', *The Atlantic*, June 2012, http://www.theatlantic.com/magazine/archive/2012/06/the-vietnam-solution/308969/.

6  Admiral Robert Willard, Testimony to the Senate Armed Service Committee, February 2012.

7  *Ibid.*

8  For more details, see: Nazery Khalid, 'South China Sea: Platform for Prosperity or Arena for Altercation?', http://southchinaseastudies.org.

9  This is important as a permanent presence above the high-water mark is a key component for qualification as an island, and therefore the ability to command an EEZ of 200nm.

10  Note however that UNCLOS has no provisions on *how* to determine sovereignty over offshore islands. For the full text of UNCLOS, see: http://www.un.org/Depts/los/convention_agreements/texts/unclos/unclos_e.pdf.

11  UNCLOS, Article 58.

12  'Hu Jintao at 18th CPC National Congress Urges PRC to become "Maritime Power"', AFP, 8 November 2012.

13  US Quadrennial Defence Review Report, February 2010, p. 8, http://www.defense.gov/qdr/qdr%20as%20of%2026jan10%200700.pdf.

14  Krishna was reacting to the suggestion by a leading Chinese commentator that India was risking heavy political and economic consequences by pursuing oil and gas exploration in the region in partnership with Vietnam. 'South China Sea is the Property of the World: Krishna', *Hindustan Times*, 6 April 2012, http://www.hindustantimes.com/India-news/NewDelhi/South-China-Sea-is-property-of-world-Krishna/Article1-836372.aspx.

15  Ju Hailong, 'India Playing Long Game in South China Sea', *Global Times*, 9 April 2012, http://www.globaltimes.cn/NEWS/tabid/99/ID/703944/India-playing-long-game-in-South-China-Sea.aspx.

16  The 'go global' strategy was a campaign initiated by the Chinese government before the turn of the millennium to encourage Chinese companies to invest overseas. The aims include securing access to resources, gaining know-how and building brand recognition.

17 See, for example, this excellent edited volume of essays: Patrick Cronin (ed.), *Cooperation from Strength: The United States, China, and the South China Sea* (Washington DC: CNAS, January 2012). Available at: http://www.cnas. org/files/documents/publications/ CNAS_CooperationFromStrength_ Cronin_1.pdf.

18 Speech by Robert Gates, IISS Shangri-La Dialogue, 30 May 2009. Available at: http://www.iiss. org/conferences/the-shangri-la-dialogue/shangri-la-dialogue-2009/ plenary-session-speeches-2009/ f i r s t - p l e n a r y - s e s s i o n / dr-robert-gates/.

19 Although some legal disputes relating to the interpretation or application of the provisions of UNCLOS appear still to be subject to the compulsory binding dispute settlement under Part XV.

20 For one example of a broadly positive assessment of these trends, and the cooperative impact of globalisation and overlapping economic interests, see: Till, 'The South China Sea: An International History', paper presented to the conference 'The South China Sea: Towards a Cooperative Management Regime', RSIS, Singapore, 16–17 May 2007. The full conference report is available at: http://www.rsis.edu.sg/ publications/conference_reports/ South_China_Sea_Report.pdf.

21 Retired US Navy Admiral Patrick Walsh suggested as much when he labelled the South China Sea a 'strategic pivot' in his interview with a Japanese newspaper: Yoichi Kato, 'Patrick Walsh: South China Sea could be a New "Strategic Pivot"', *Asahi Shimbun*, 21 March 2012, http://ajw.asahi.com/article/ asia/china/AJ201203210024.

22 Kaplan argues that this is 'not necessarily war, not necessarily an outbreak of military hostilities, but a lot of jockeying for position, a lot of brinksmanship, a lot of to-ing and fro-ing of warships'. Kaplan, 'The South China Sea is the Future of Conflict', *Foreign Policy*, September–October 2012. Meanwhile, Brendan Taylor argues that the South China Sea is a 'strategic backwater' rather than a potential flashpoint of any consequence, in contrast, for example, to the nuclear undertones to instability on the Korean Peninsula or the Taiwan Strait. Taylor, 'Storm in a Teacup over South China Sea', *The Australian*, 11 May 2012, http:// w w w . t h e a u s t r a l i a n . c o m . a u / opinion/world-commentary/storm-in-teacup-over-south-china-sea/ story-e6frg6ux-1226352425072.

23 Peter Dutton, 'Cracks in the Global Foundation: International Law and Instability in the South China Sea', in Cronin (ed.), *Cooperation from Strength*, pp. 69–81.

# CHAPTER ONE

# Mapping the history

No territorial dispute is as confusing, as confounding and as complex as that of the South China Sea. The disagreements within the 3.7 million square kilometres of water involve multiple states drawing on contested historical records with occasionally ambiguous claims and questionable legal interpretations. The situation is further complicated by the presence in the region in the eighteenth and nineteenth century of European colonial powers, who exercised suzerainty or outright sovereignty over large swathes of this territory, and hence bequeathed claims in the South China Sea to their post-colonial successor states.

Despite this complex background, mapping the disputes and their historical basis is vital in any analysis of the reasons for the current tensions in the region. A detailed assessment of the claims and counter-claims, and their respective histories, helps provide the context in which current tensions are unfolding.

The convolution of the South China Sea disputes is reflected in the range of nomenclature deployed to describe the assorted features contained therein. One state's Amboyna Cay is another state's Lagos, Anbo Shazhou, Dao An Bang or Pulau Amboyna Kecil.[1] Similarly, defining exactly which features lie within each island group is not without its dangers, while one of the most contentious issues in delimiting sovereignty in the sea is pinpointing exactly which features remain above the sea at high tide and can sustain human habitation (thereby qualifying as islands with an international legal right to EEZs) and those which do not.[2]

## The law and the sea

As has already been set out in the introduction, the South China Sea is a strategic node, not only for its busy shipping lanes, but also because of its substantial fish stocks and potential hydrocarbon and mineral wealth. Securing this wealth provides a considerable incentive for all littoral states to stake claims within the region. But it is not the sea itself that is really in dispute, but rather the islands scattered throughout it. According to international treaties and customary law, all claims to sovereignty and rights at sea must ultimately start on land.

The primary instrument for delimiting and regulating claims of sovereignty and rights at sea is UNCLOS. This convention was an attempt to formalise the centuries-old customary maritime law, which drew heavily on Hugo Grotius's concepts of *mare liberum* and the idea of another Dutch jurist, Cornelius van Bijnkershoek, that a territorial sea extended out to the maximum range of the most effective weaponry, so as to allow nations to exercise effective control over their waters.[3]

The current iteration of UNCLOS hails from the third meeting of the UN Conference on the Law of the Sea, which involved discussions that lasted nearly a decade, from 1973 until 1982. This conference, and the resulting convention, stated that all coastal states had the right to a territorial water zone extending out 12 nautical miles from agreed baselines (the low-water line along the coast and around islands) and an EEZ extending 200 nautical miles from these baselines. The territorial sea is essentially sovereign territory: the coastal state can set laws regulating maritime traffic and exploit all resources within or underneath the seas. In addition, foreign naval vessels may only be in these waters by agreement or if undergoing 'innocent passage', while submarines must transit territorial waters surfaced and with their flag showing. In the EEZ, the coastal state has the sovereign right to exploit all sea and undersea resources, but does not exercise sovereignty over the territory: there are no restrictions on maritime traffic, even for warships.[4]

The relevance of all this legalese to the South China Sea is that territorial seas and EEZs can extend not just from a coastline, but also from islands, however remote. So, for example, the Falkland Islands provides the UK with an EEZ of over 550,872km² in the South Atlantic, including some potentially lucrative oil deposits within those waters. In the South China Sea, those features deemed to be habitable islands could theoretically provide hundreds of thousands of square kilometres of sea and seabed resources for exploitation (China and Taiwan, for instance, have variously been interpreted as claiming anywhere between two million km² and 80% of the sea, or 2.95 million km²). For the energy- and fish-hungry nations of East Asia, this is a sizeable catch.

Then there is the problem of defining exactly which features qualify as islands under UNCLOS, and which of those islands are, in turn, habitable. An island – defined by UNCLOS as naturally formed, surrounded by water and above water at high tide – is entitled to a territorial sea, contiguous zone, EEZ and continental shelf. However, if an island is merely a formation of rocks that is unable to sustain human habitation or economic life in its own right, it is only entitled to a territorial sea, and not to an EEZ or continental shelf. At a conservative estimate, of the hundreds of features in the Spratly Islands, perhaps 33 of them lie above the sea, and only seven of them have an area exceeding 0.5km².[5]

One further final complication is that states can claim exclusive rights over the seabed and subsoil and its resources beyond the 200nm EEZ limit if it can be proven that the seabed forms part of the state's continental shelf. Vietnam and Malaysia have made an official claim to an extended continental shelf in the South China Sea, while Brunei has also stated that its continental shelf extends beyond the standard 200 nautical miles, but has yet officially to delineate its proposed extent.

## Clarifying the claims today

Although there are six disputants to the South China Sea, there are in essence only five different claims. China and Taiwan share an all but identical claim. Whilst they claim all of the islands in the South China Sea, Vietnam claims the entirety of the Paracel and Spratly archipelagos – although it has not specified precisely which islands it includes in these groupings. The Philippines claims Scarborough Reef and the Kalayaan Island group, both of which are in the eastern reaches of the South China Sea and the latter of which consists of 53 features that form most of the Spratly archipelago. Malaysia claims 11 features in the Spratly Islands – all in the southern section, where it currently occupies eight (the other three are occupied by the Philippines and Vietnam).[6] Malaysia also claims the numerous Luconia Shoals and James Shoal, which sit within the Sino-Taiwanese nine-dashed line, but there is little diplomatic weight given to these features. Lastly, Brunei claims two features, the partially submerged Louisa Reef (occupied by

Malaysia) and the entirely submerged Rifleman Bank (which has a raised platform constructed and occupied by Vietnam on its northernmost extremity, Bombay Castle).[7]

When it comes to occupations, as opposed to the simple registration of claims, Vietnam is the most active of the six disputants, currently occupying 27 features in the Spratly Islands.[8] China has occupied seven features in the Spratly Islands, but has also some form of physical occupation on nine of the Paracels and controls them in their entirety. The Philippines has occupied nine features (although one is essentially a rusting tanker ran aground at Second Thomas Shoal)[9] and Malaysia has control of eight Spratly features (although it is unclear whether there is any permanent occupation beyond markers at Louisa and Royal Charlotte Reefs and whether the historically reported presence on Dallas Reef is permanent). Taiwan has taken one of the Spratly Islands (Itu Aba), although it nominally controls Ban Than Reef and sent its first Environmental Protection Administration sample collection team there in 2010.[10] It also controls the Pratas Island – the only significant island in the Pratas Island grouping. Brunei is the only claimant with no record of occupations.

Yet the precise nature of the claims made by these disputants is not always clear, neither in their extent nor in their legal or historical underpinnings. Perhaps the most infamous example of this ambiguity is the Sino-Taiwanese claim, which is based on the same nine-dashed line and which extends in an approximation of a cow's tongue down into much of the sea, appearing to encompass all the islands therein as well as around 80% of the water. The precise significance of this nine-dashed line remains unclear. Does it indicate a claim to all of the waters inside the line – which would be in clear contravention of the articles and principles of UNCLOS – or only the habitable islands within this area, and the UNCLOS-designated territorial and EEZs extending from these landmasses? Chinese officialdom has shown a distinct distaste for clarification since inheriting the map from the Kuomintang (KMT) in 1949 (although it was first published in 1947, and then as an 11-dashed line). The closest they have come to clarification was in a rare official submission of the map attached to a *Note Verbale* submitted by China to the UN secretary-general on 7 May 2009, which stated that China 'has indisputable sovereignty over the islands in the South China Sea and the adjacent waters, and enjoys sovereign rights and jurisdiction over the relevant waters as well as the seabed and subsoil thereof'.[11] Whilst the phraseology is somewhat strange (what, for instance, are 'adjacent waters'?), this note would appear to indicate that China's claim now emanates from the land features contained within the nine-dashed line, rather than being a claim to all its water.

China's *Note Verbale* was submitted in response to a joint submission by Vietnam and Malaysia to the UN's Commission on the Limits of the Continental Shelf (CLCS), and was part of a flurry of official diplomatic documents that made for a particularly enlightening period in terms of clarifying many of the respective claims. The catalyst for this burst of diplomatic activity was a deadline of 13 May 2009 for the states in Southeast Asia to submit to the CLCS if they intended to make a claim for a continental shelf beyond the standard 200 nautical miles provided for under UNCLOS. Shortly before this deadline, in February 2009, the Philippines, for example, passed the Archipelagic Baselines Law, defining its baselines (and hence its 200nm EEZ) and also laying claim to a large proportion of the Spratly Islands (known as the Kalayaan Island Group in the Philippines) and Scarborough Reef.[12] This law was followed by the government's deposit of a list of coordinates of its baselines with the UN secretary-general, clearly outlining Philippine claims.

## Understanding where these claims come from

The question remains, how did we arrive at this complicated mosaic of overlapping claims and intermingled occupations, which has involved rival disputants militarily occupying tiny islets as close as three kilometres apart?[13] The answer is fascinatingly complex, involving regional powers, colonial states, private individuals and corporate interests.

### From ancient to modern

For centuries, fishermen, salvagers and small trade vessels from the littoral countries comprised the vast majority of traffic in the South China Sea, whilst leaving the islands themselves largely uninhabited. This backdrop has allowed China, Taiwan and Vietnam, in particular, all to seek to bolster their island claims with allusions to the principles of discovery, 'historic rights' and occupation, suggesting that their populations were the first to find the islands, regularly used them as waypoints or shelter and as such had de facto occupied them. These countries also use their long imperial histories to suggest that military patrols, surveys and geographical markers were made or left by their political ancestors, thereby demonstrating continued sovereignty over these islands.[14] However, given the paucity of the official records over this issue, the difficulty of communications and the lack of evidence of continuous occupation and sovereignty, it is problematic for any disputant to prove their superior entitlement clearly. While there are official records of Nguyen Emperor Minh Mang ordering the construction of a temple and stele on the Paracel Islands in 1835, for example, information on previous imperial interactions with the islands derives from maps and testimony from foreign missionaries and counsellors. This is perhaps unsurprising: the tenets of contemporary international law could not have been foreseen by previous administrations in the

Asian states, and hence the idea of prioritising physical occupation of an island over simply restating one's sovereignty
infrequently would have seemed unnecessary. Furthermore,
the constantly shifting boundaries of the states in Asia, which
were buffeted by neighbours as empires rose and fell, further
obscures historical records, and helps explain why there may
have been a lack of consistency to assertions by claimant states
over time. Finally, the intervention of European imperial
powers from the sixteenth century, in particular the influence
of France in Vietnam and Japan from the nineteenth century,
further confused the situation with the issue of succession
from colonial power to former colony.[15]

### Extra-regional powers compete (1925–1945)

The modern story of the South China Sea disputes begins in
the twentieth century. Prior to this, governments tended to
be too weak, fragmented or colonised to follow through on
their respective claims of sovereignty. Yet, by the twentieth
century, assertions of sovereignty were beginning to mount.
For example, in 1902 and again in 1908, the then-fading
Qing empire sent missions under Rear Admiral Li Zhun
to claim the Paracels. Although no occupation was established, Li recommended in his 1909 report that the islands
should be administered by Hainan Island; five years later a
map was published by cartographer Hu Jinjie that showed a
U-shaped line around the Paracels. In 1921, Guangdong province awarded a permit to develop the Paracels to a Cantonese
merchant, Ho Jui-nien (presumably Ho Ruinian in pinyin),
who duly proceeded to develop a phosphate-processing centre
on Woody Island.[16] In 1928, a commission was appointed to
investigate the Paracels, which were described by the head
of the commission Shen Peng-fei as 'our nation's southernmost territory'.[17] By 1935, China's recently promulgated Land

and Water Maps Inspection Committee was ruling that its southernmost territory should reach the 4°N latitude line, encompassing James Shoal. An edited cartographical volume published in 1936, as the *New Map of Chinese Construction*, included a *Map of Chinese Domain in the South China Sea*, which for the first time showed the boundaries of China extending to below James Shoal. It declared that the islands claimed by France – Macclesfield Bank and the Spratly Islands – were 'the living places of Chinese fishermen' and hence 'sovereignty, of course, belonged to China'.[18]

The Chinese administration of the Paracels and Ho's exploitation of the phosphate there had been watched with interest by France, including through two visits by a French military vessel in 1925 and 1926. In 1929, and without prior permission from Paris, the French governor of Cochinchina ordered the warship *Malicieuse* to take formal possession of Spratly Island and 'the islets depending on it'.[19] Paris subsequently followed up this *fait accompli* with a claim to a rectangular area of the South China Sea that encompassed much of the Spratly Islands. Japan officially protested, and the UK consul general in Saigon reported to London that the French must have made a mistake, appearing unaware of a claim the British had made since 1877 to Spratly Island and Amboyna Cay. The feeble British protest which followed was indicative of the sanguine attitude to the islands of the day, perceived as they were as having little commercial or strategic interest. Yet France continued to bolster its claim and, in July 1933, published a proclamation of annexation in the *Journal Officiel* naming six islands: Spratly Island, Amboyna Cay, Itu Aba, North Danger Reef (which comprises Northeast and Southwest Cays, as well as North and South Reef), Loaita Bank and Thitu. In July 1938, Paris finally declared ownership of the Paracels as well and created a delegation under the governor of Cochinchina.[20]

These incidents aside, a generally lackadaisical approach to the South China Sea could be explained on the part of Asian countries by their weak governments and lack of military power projection or by their colonial status, and on the part of European powers by their lack of strategic interest in these small features amid more pressing concerns in *Mitteleuropa*. The islands provided little commercial interest beyond convenient layover points for fishing vessels and extensive guano deposits. However, one factor began to change the position of European states towards the sea: the rise and expansion of imperial Japan.

Japan's interests in the South China Sea began as commercial or private ventures. In 1907, Japanese explorer Nishizawa Yoshiji occupied Pratas Island on his own behalf with 100 supporters, but was persuaded to depart the following year after a large indemnity was paid by China.[21] Japanese covert exploitation of phosphate in the Paracels was undertaken from 1919, with Ho's exploits there in fact bankrolled by a Taiwan-based, Japanese-owned organisation, with the phosphate then exported to Japan. But by the 1930s, Japan's interests in the South China Sea had begun to migrate from the commercial to the military. Imperial Japan had already colonised Taiwan (then Formosa) in 1895, Korea in 1905 and Manchuria from 1933. In 1937, with its campaign in war-ravaged China gathering pace, its attentions also started to focus southwards. In September of that year, Japan occupied Pratas Island in the South China Sea. Alarmed, the UK developed a proposal to lease either Itu Aba or Thitu from France in order to develop an airfield, while the Philippines suggested to the US that it should occupy the Spratlys. Neither proposal had any impact; the relentless expansion of Japan continued. It occupied Woody, Spratly and Lincoln islands in early 1938. In early 1939, Japan landed on Hainan Island and in April claimed sovereignty over all of the Paracel and Spratly Islands, leading to protests from both London and Paris.

However, as war broke out with the West, the success of the Imperial Japanese Forces ensured there was little either European power could do to prevent the occupation of the South China Sea, including the construction of a submarine base on Itu Aba and a radio base on Namyit Island.

### From the international to the regional (1945–1970)

The end of the Second World War saw a temporary demilitari-sation of much of the South China Sea. Japan renounced all its titles and claims to the Spratly and Paracel Islands under the San Francisco Treaty of September 1951, while France had, by this point, already been ousted from the Spratlys and drawn back from the Paracels, and was increasingly mired in irregular warfare against the Viet Minh. The South China Sea islands were therefore for the most part essentially unoccupied, a *tabula rasa* – a fact confirmed by French frigate *Escarmouche* and minesweeper *Chevreuil* in two separate surveys in 1946.[22]

Over the course of the next decade, the main protagonists claiming the islands shifted from being extra-regional actors, like Japan and France, to the littoral states of the South China Sea.[23] Meanwhile, the interests of the governments of these littoral states began increasingly to be supported by their own developing abilities to project power into the sea and by a nascent codified international system. Regional parties looked not only to project and sustain their forces into the South China Sea, but also to administer the islands and claims bureaucratically. For example, in late 1955, China reoccupied Woody Island in the eastern Paracels, assuming occupation of the feature from Taiwan, which had abandoned it five years previously, following the KMT's retreat from the mainland. Meanwhile, as French forces withdrew from Vietnam in 1956, so the South Vietnamese presence in the western Paracels remained (the 'French' detachment had in fact been southern Vietnamese paramilitaries under French administration). The Paracels were thus occupied by two entities: China in the eastern group and South Vietnam in the western.

In May 1956 a further party entered the fray, in perhaps one of the more unusual stories behind the complex South China Sea tales. Filipino millionaire businessman and lawyer Tomas Cloma, with support from his brother Filemon and approximately 30 accomplices, landed on Thitu Island and Itu Aba and claimed 53 features west of Palawan as 'Kalayaan' (Tagalog for Freedomland). Tomas issued a 'Notice to the Whole World' that Freedomland was an independent state, basing his claim on the fact that the islands were uninhabited and hence the principles of *res nullius* and 'discovery'. China and Taiwan predictably protested vigorously, with the latter sending three flotillas to the region between June and September. Now alerted to the dangers of foreign occupation, by late 1956 Taiwan had reoccupied Itu Aba.

The Cloma brothers acted independently, whilst a Philippine special interdepartmental committee determined at this point that the islands closest to the Philippines were unowned, unoccupied, unsurveyed and unclaimed. It was not until 1971 that Manila officially claimed Kalayaan and just the year before that it sent troops to the Spratlys to occupy its first features.[24] Nevertheless the Clomas's claims and the incident this sparked appears to have persuaded South Vietnam not only to reiterate its claims to the Paracels but also, for the first time, claim the Spratly Islands as the successor to France's earlier imperial claim. China also reiterated its claim in its 1958 Declaration on China's Territorial Sea, which mentioned the Xisha (Paracel), Dongsha (Pratas), Zhongsha (Macclesfield Bank/Scarborough Reef) and Nansha (Spratly) islands as all being sovereign Chinese territory.

### The sea runs red (1970–1995)

By the early 1970s, the situation in the South China Sea was beginning to resemble the mosaic of claims on display there today. China, Taiwan, South Vietnam and the Philippines had all laid out their claims, to a greater or lesser extent. Although Malaysia would not follow suit until 1979, with the publication of the expansively named *Peta Baru Menunjukkan Sempadan Perairan dan Pelantar Benua Malysia*,[25] the South China Sea disputes had essentially moved into a new phase. With claims and initial occupations now ventured, parties began to press militarily for the best possible position in the sea. The primary goal of this activity was to bolster each disputant's claim to sovereignty and administration, while naturally denying the possibility to others. An ancillary objective was to create the best possible negotiating position for any future consultations that might occur.

Whilst moves to bolster their respective positions were largely enacted through the occupation of uninhabited features and the expansion of existing outposts, the potential spoils on offer occasionally overrode concerns to avoid military conflict. For example, the coupling of the oil-price spike of 1973 with a growing awareness of the possibility of hydrocarbon resources in the region brought new economic incentives for claimants to expand their territorial interests in the South China Sea.[26] Meanwhile, the international arena was ripe for an emboldened China to push its influence and position in the region: South Vietnam was engaged in the final throes of its war with North Vietnam; the US had, by August 1973, withdrawn its combat forces from the Indochinese quagmire; the US-supported collective defence organisation, the Southeast Asia Treaty Organisation (SEATO), was close to dissolution while ASEAN was only a nascent body; and China was enjoying its recent rapprochement with Washington.

The result, in January 1974, was the Battle of the Paracels between China and South Vietnam. Faced with Chinese encroachment into the Crescent group in the form of People's Liberation Army (PLA) troops and supporting vessels, specifically on Robert and Money Islands, Saigon sent a flotilla of former US Navy and Coast Guard vessels to evict them.[27] Initial attempts to negotiate soon descended into a gun battle that lasted just 35 minutes before both sides retreated to their ports, with the Chinese forces sustaining fewer casualties.[28] Yet, whereas China then followed up by dispatching a number of MiG-21s, a cruiser and two submarines to the area, Saigon, with support from the US not forthcoming, opted against escalating what seemed increasingly like a lost cause. Over the following days, China occupied the former South Vietnamese position on Pattle Island and with it, assumed effective control over the Crescent group and hence the entire Paracel archipelago.

The Chinese victory in the Paracels had two immediate effects. First, with the competition for control over the archipelago eliminated, China was free to fortify its positions there. Today, Beijing maintains outposts throughout the Paracels: in the southwestern Crescent group – formerly occupied by Vietnam – the primary occupation is on Pattle Island, but China also maintains a presence on Money and Drummond Islands, as well as a small harbour and outpost on the remote sandbank of Triton Island. In the northeastern Amphitrite group, by far the largest occupation is on Woody Island, where a 2.7km airstrip has been constructed on the 1.5km-wide island (nearly half the airstrip is constructed on reclaimed land). This is now linked to Rocky Island by a raised road. China has also built a small harbour and outpost on Lincoln Island, as well as minor outposts on Tree and North Islands.

The second consequence of China's victory in the Paracels was to encourage greater competition elsewhere in the South

China Sea. For example, the perceived expansionism of China incentivised South Vietnam to multiply and consolidate its occupations in the Spratly Islands, which in turn inspired other regional states to do the same for fear that they would permanently lose title to the islands in the face of Vietnam's dominant occupation. Thus, between 1974 and 1975 alone, South Vietnam occupied five further features, including one that was already occupied by the Philippines.[29] In April 1975, as the civil war came to an end, North Vietnam not only occupied the features in the Spratlys then held by South Vietnam, but continued expanding its interests in the sea more broadly, adding Central London Reef to its collection in 1978. The Philippines similarly increased its holdings in the 1970s. Having started its occupations in the early 1970s, by 1974 Manila occupied at least five features (Flat Island, Nanshan Island, Northeast Cay, Thitu Island and West York Island), with a small and perhaps non-permanent presence on Southwest Cay arguably to be considered a sixth. In the mid-1970s, the Philippines suffered a setback with its bloodless eviction by Vietnam from Southwest Cay. It went on, however, to occupy a further two features in 1978 (Lankiam Cay and Loaita Island). It also subsequently occupied Commodore Reef, as well as entrenching its position on the larger islands it already held.[30]

Meanwhile, Malaysia's publication of its map in 1979 effectively opened its campaign for sovereignty in the region, with the 1980s characterised by its occupation of various features covered by its claims. Its first move came in Swallow Reef, which it occupied in 1983, followed by Ardasier Reef and Marivales Reef in 1986, and Dallas Reef and Louisa Reef in 1987.[31]

Having asserted its dominance in the Paracel Islands and fought a brief but intense border war with Vietnam in 1979, Beijing had paid scant attention to the rush for territory in the Spratlys. However, aware that it was rapidly losing a window of opportunity to bolster its claims there with demonstrable occupation, in 1987 China sent a naval survey to the islands. This survey was followed up by a rapid occupation by China of features in the Spratlys from February 1988.

Once again, China's moves took place against a favourable international backdrop. The external influence of the Soviet Union was clearly on the wane, to the extent that its withdrawal from its Southeast Asian base at Cam Ranh in Vietnam was being publicly discussed. The US was still hurting from its humiliation in Vietnam and focused on developments in the Soviet Union. Meanwhile, Vietnam was contemplating its withdrawal from Cambodia after a decade of occupation following its ousting of the Khmer Rouge in 1979 – an operation which had further isolated Hanoi from China and the US.

When a second major clash between China and Vietnam in the South China Sea occurred, therefore, China was again able to bet against Vietnam finding much external support. With Vietnam also increasing the tempo of its occupations in response to Chinese moves, confrontation ensued. In the most serious violence in the South China Sea since the Second World War, the battle at Johnson South Reef cost the lives of 74 Vietnamese sailors. China successfully thwarted Vietnamese plans to occupy the reef and went on to consolidate its position on six islands in the Spratlys that year alone.[32] Vietnam, meanwhile, was able over the period 1987–91 to occupy a further string of features, easily becoming the most active disputant in terms of occupations in the South China Sea. Indeed, it is notable that all of the features occupied during this period by Vietnam are in fact partially or wholly submerged reefs and sandbanks, suggesting that Vietnam had run out of islets to occupy and was forced to build artificial constructions on submerged cement foundations in order to sustain these outposts.[33]

This dynamic of occupations continued into the 1990s. In 1995, a Philippines reconnaissance flight noted Chinese structures on wooden stilts being built on Mischief Reef. Although Manila protested, the structures continued to be fortified and strengthened, leading to the current situation where a multi-storey structure built on concrete foundations along with several buildings on stilts are able to house up to 50 PLAN marines.[34] Meanwhile Taiwan began a construction project on Ban Than Reef in 1995 (and even bothered to build a birdwatching stand there in 2004);[35] Malaysia built on Erica Reef in 1998 and Louisa Reef in 1999, the same year in which the Philippines sent naval personnel to Second Thomas Reef. However, the major waves of expansion in the South China Sea were by the mid-1990s completed, as all the disputants bar Brunei satisfied themselves that they were able to bolster their claims with evidence of occupation.

**From competition to co-operation... (1995–2005)**
It was in this situation that diplomacy rather than irredentism, annexation and occupation was belatedly able to come to the fore in the South China Sea disputes – albeit alongside a continued if quieter dynamic of fortification. During the period of expansion from the 1970s until the 1990s, the key points of tension often flowed from actions instigated by China, albeit on occasion as a result of perceived aggression emanating from elsewhere. So it was in the period from the mid-1990s that China again had a key role to play in the determination of a more cooperative atmosphere. Of course, it helped that Beijing had by now managed to muscle its way into controlling the entire Paracels and occupying seven reefs in the Spratly Islands (not to mention the 'Chinese' occupations of Itu Aba and Pratas through Taipei), but China was also embarking on a broader charm offensive in Southeast Asia.

Beijing's management of the Asian financial crisis of 1997–1998 highlighted its increasing interests in closer Southeast Asian relations. Amid the currency collapses that began with the Thai baht and spiralled into a regional crisis, China resisted pressure to devalue its currency, thereby helping stabilise the situation and preventing the spread of further contagion. The result was significant goodwill among Southeast Asian states towards the seemingly responsible monetary policies from the north.

Meanwhile, Southeast Asian interests in diplomacy were encouraged by the entry in July 1995 of Vietnam into ASEAN as its seventh member. With all four Southeast Asian claimant states now members of the same regional body, a more multilateral approach could be explored. At least in theory, the idea was that ASEAN could help Southeast Asian claimants engage Beijing on a more equal basis, thereby escaping the constraints of their asymmetric bilateral relations. Already in 1992, ASEAN had issued a declaration on the South China Sea urging the parties to resolve the disputes peacefully and suggesting for the first time a code of conduct to regulate behaviour there.[36] Then in 1995, following their stand-off at Mischief Reef, China and the Philippines signed a bilateral eight-point agreement pledging a peaceful approach to dispute management. Months later, Vietnam and the Philippines signed a nine-point agreement along similar lines.

As a fashion for statements pledging cooperation took hold, so the most celebrated of these emerged; in November 2002 a Declaration on the Conduct of Parties in the South China Sea (DoC) was signed by all ten ASEAN members and China. The ten-point declaration reaffirmed that the parties would resolve their differences peacefully, in accordance with UNCLOS, and refrain from inhabiting further features. It also supposedly committed all parties to work towards the agreement of a more legally enforceable Code of Conduct. Whilst the DoC did not appear to deter the various parties from strengthening or even expanding existing fortifications, it did nevertheless reflect a change of mood in the region from one of outright competition to one of calmer dialogue.

This greater sense of self-restraint and mutual cooperation was further reflected in China's signature, in October 2003, of the Treaty of Amity and Co-operation – an ASEAN document in which parties agreed not to engage in activity that posed a threat to the stability or sovereignty of another party and to settle all disputes through friendly negotiations.

Finally, in March 2005, a trilateral agreement was signed between China, Vietnam and the Philippines. The Joint Marine Seismic Undertaking (JMSU) committed the three parties, through their major oil and gas companies, to explore jointly an area spanning more than 142,000km$^2$ in the South China Sea. Although the agreement did not mention profit sharing should hydrocarbon riches be found, it did seem to raise the genuine possibility that regional states would be able to shelve their dispute and begin exploitation of the sea's resources for mutual benefit.

### ....and back again (2005–present)

Yet it was not to be. The JMSU ran its three-year course and expired without extension, after an embattled Philippine administration came under heavy criticism for the location of the exploration area within Philippines-claimed Kalayaan, and faced allegations of unconstitutionality that included the charge that the JMSU was a Chinese condition for favourable loans.

At about the same time and in a clear indication of renewed expansion of facilities in the South China Sea, in January 2008, Taiwan inaugurated a 1,150m-long airstrip on Itu Aba Island. All occupying entities now had airstrips on at least one feature in the Spratly Islands (Taiwan already had a runway on Pratas Island). While the facade of cooperation may still have been present through the 2002 DoC, it was increasingly clear that the fundamental underlying lack of trust among the parties was continuing to encourage the militarisation of these disputes in particular and the region in general.

Three events in 2009 gave the lie to an era of apparent cooperation in the South China Sea and contributed to a rapid souring of regional relations. One was the aforementioned May 2009 CLCS deadline for extended continental shelf claims. The submissions, notes and counter-notes that resulted both reflected and reinvigorated tensions involved in the management of the sea's disputes.[37] A second was the USNS *Impeccable* incident of March 2009, whereby a US Military Sealift Command vessel was harassed by five Chinese paramilitary and civilian vessels, forcing it to stop and protect its towed sonar array.[38] Although this was not the first instance of Chinese forces attempting to prevent US surveillance (the 2001 Hainan EP-3 incident and the 2002 USNS *Bowditch* incident in the Yellow Sea were just two of the more public further examples), the fact that it occurred in the run-up to the CLCS submissions and amidst increasingly confident demonstrations of naval power by China in its near-abroad magnified its importance, thereby further underlining the narrative of a Chinese return towards more coercive diplomacy in the South China Sea. Finally, the July 2009 testimony by Scot Marciel, deputy assistant secretary in the US Bureau of East Asian and Pacific Affairs, to the US Senate Foreign Relations Committee publicised what had long been suspected: that Beijing had been putting foreign oil companies under pressure to stop work on joint exploration projects in disputed waters.[39]

This confirmation of harassment of foreign oil companies came against a background whereby in just two years, between 2006 and 2007, Beijing had issued 18 objections to the involvement of foreign companies in concessions awarded by Vietnam.[40] A US diplomatic cable from Hanoi dated from July 2007, and released by WikiLeaks in 2011, also suggested that the Chinese covert campaign against foreign oil companies had begun in 2006 and that, by 2007, four US and eight foreign companies had been targeted, with five deals suspended or cancelled.[41] As diplomatic demarches proved ineffective at halting hydrocarbon ventures in disputed waters and Chinese concern grew over a concerted strategy by first Vietnam and subsequently the Philippines to attract more international attention to the South China Sea disputes, so further escalation followed. In February 2011, Philippine fishing boats 140nm from Palawan were ordered to leave the area by a PLAN frigate, which threatened to fire, while in March a Philippine-contracted survey vessel, MV *Veritas Voyager*, was forced to suspend its operations after two Chinese paramilitary vessels threatened to ram it.[42] Meanwhile, in two separate incidents in quick succession in May–June 2011, Vietnam accused China of using paramilitary vessels, in the first instance, and fishing vessels, in the second, to attempt to cut the sonar array being towed by vessels contracted by PetroVietnam to explore for oil in the South China Sea.

China's actions, while seen by Beijing as legitimate reactions to provocative hydrocarbon exploration by Vietnam and the Philippines, quickly generated concern in its Southeast Asian neighbours and further afield. When combined with the coercive economic diplomacy evident during the rare earths export embargo placed on Japan in 2010 and a banana import embargo placed on the Philippines in 2012 in reaction to a stand-off between China and the Philippines at Scarborough Reef, these events suggested that an emboldened Beijing was now pursuing a more 'assertive' policy in its near-abroad. Certainly the

US Senate appeared to agree, passing a resolution in June 2011 condemning China for its 'use of force' in the South China Sea.[43]

Recent history also therefore suggests that Chinese activities have been setting the tempo and nature of developments in the South China Sea. For example, as criticisms of Chinese assertiveness mounted and as some Southeast Asian nations reacted in part by seeking closer engagement with the US, so China again dialled back on its rhetoric and reaction. As it sought to reassure regional partners and minimise US openings for its 'pivot' to Asia, so a tactical and rhetorical reminder of the need for cooperation became once more an attractive option. So it was that, at the height of the furore over cable cutting, China and ASEAN were able to agree a set of Guidelines for the Implementation of the Declaration on Conduct of Parties in July 2011. With little new in terms of content, the goal of agreement on a Code of Conduct which these guidelines reiterated remains, at the time of writing, elusive. Even as and when such a code is forthcoming, those wishing to assess its impact will need to look beyond its simple issuance to its substance. Is it legally binding, is it enforceable, is the language tight and the way forward clear? Or will obfuscation and convenient generalities remain the order of the day?

Given its size, regional influence and expansive claims in the sea, China remains the arbiter of the pace and future of such agreements. This burden of responsibility in the South China Sea may, perhaps, be unwanted, but it has only increased in line with Beijing's growing economic influence and military might and this pattern is unlikely to change. It is therefore to China that this book turns first to examine its behaviours, motivations and decision-making processes in the handling of these historically complex and legally involved disputes.

# Notes

1   Amboyna Cay is the English name for a Vietnamese-occupied Spratly Island, known in Tagalog as Lagos, in Chinese as Anbo Shazhou, in Vietnamese as Đào An Bang and in Malay as Pulau Amboyna Kecil.

2   For a description of which maritime features qualify for EEZs, see: UNCLOS, Article 121.

3   Hugo Grotius's *Mare Liberum*, published in 1609, clearly outlined the principle that the oceans were international territory and free to be used by all nations for seaborne trade. This could be seen as a reaction to the Iberian principles of monopolistic trade with the then burgeoning Portuguese and Spanish empires, which greatly hindered Dutch merchants. Van Bijnkershoek added practicality to Grotius's principles, by declaring that 'terrae potestas finitur ubi finitur armorum vis' [territory ends where the force of arms ends]. This, generally, although not universally, came to be accepted as three miles, the maximum range of the most advanced early eighteenth-century cannon.

4   According to UNCLOS, the waters of the EEZ are subject to the same articles and principles of freedom of navigation as the high seas. This means there are no restrictions on overflight and navigation, but they are reserved for peaceful purposes. This latter point (enshrined in Article 88) has, in addition to Article 58 that mentions the 'due regard' to be accorded to the regulations of the coastal state, led to a disagreement in the interpretation of the text, with China in particular suggesting that military surveillance is not peaceful and therefore violates this article.

5   Ji Guoxing, *Maritime Jurisdiction in the Three China Seas: Options for Equitable Settlement* (San Diego, CA: University of California Institute on Global Conflict and Cooperation, 1995), p. 14. Sources vary on the number of features in the Spratlys. The highest approximation suggests 148 named features in the Spratlys, and around 400 features in total (many of which are entirely submerged). Hancox and Prescott have 125 separate named features. David Hancox and Victor Prescott, 'A Geographic Description of the Spratly Islands and an Account of Hyrdrographic Surveys Amongst those Islands', IBRU *Maritime Briefings*, vol. 1, no. 6, 1995.

6   The eight Malaysian-occupied features are Amboyna Cay, Ardasier Reef, Barque Canada Reef, Commodore Reef, Dallas Reef, Erica Reef, Investigator Reef, Louisa Reef, Mariveles Reef, Royal Charlotte Reef and Swallow Reef.

7   For a fuller explanation of current claims and the 2009 CLCS submissions, see: Robert Beckman and Tara Davenport, 'CLCS Submissions and Claims in the South China Sea', *Second International Workshop on The South China Sea: Cooperation for Regional Security and Development*, Ho Chi Minh City, 10–12 November 2010.

8   Although various sources claim Vietnam also occupied a further feature, Grierson Reef, satellite imagery does not suggest any permanent occupation.

[9] 'Philippines Grapples with Territorial Defense in Disputed Spratlys', *Kyodo News*, 17 June 2012.

[10] 'Water Quality of Spratly Islands' Ban Than Reef Measured for the First Time', *Environmental Policy Monthly*, vol. 13, no. 11, http://www.epa.gov.tw/FileLink/FileHandler.ashx?file=14523.

[11] Note of China No. CLM/172009.

[12] Republic Act No. 387, 'An Act to Amend Certain Provisions of Republic Act No. 3046'. As Amended by Republic Act 5446, to 'Define the Archipelagic Baselines of the Philippines, and for Other Purposes', 10 March 2009.

[13] The closest rival occupations are currently held by the Philippines (on Northeast Cay) and Vietnam (on Southwest Cay) in the North Danger Reef area of the Spratly Islands.

[14] See, for example: 'The Hoang Sa and Truong Sa Archipelagoes Vietnamese Territories', Ministry of Foreign Affairs, Socialist Republic of Vietnam, 1981; and 'China's Indisputable Sovereignty over the Xisha and Nansha Islands', Documents of the Ministry of Foreign Affairs of the People's Republic of China, 30 January 1980.

[15] The authors have omitted a possible discussion around the claim made by the Meads family, based on the purported 'discovery' of the Spratly Islands by Captain James George Meads, a British citizen and master of the *Modeste*. Related claims to the related Republic of Morac-Songhrati-Meads and the Kingdom of Humanity appear now to be moribund given the death of all remaining claimant individuals in a shipwreck in 1972 (ironically, in the South China Sea).

[16] A six-year bureaucratic battle ensued, as Ho attempted to gain permission for this.

[17] Marwyn S. Samuels, *Contest for the South China Sea* (New York/London: Methuen & Co, 1982), pp. 55–60 (quotation on p. 57).

[18] Jinming Li and Dexia Li, 'The Dotted Line on the Chinese Map of the South China Sea: A Note', *Ocean Development and International Law*, vol. 34, no. 3, 2003, pp. 281–95.

[19] Stein Tonneson, 'The South China Sea in the Age of European Decline', *Modern Asian Studies*, vol. 40, no. 1, February 2006, p. 5.

[20] Overviews of European and Chinese sovereignty claims in the South China Sea came from: Tonneson, 'The South China Sea in the Age of European Decline', pp. 1-57; and Samuels, *Contest for the South China Sea*, chapter 4.

[21] Dieter Heinzig, *Disputed Islands in the South China Sea* (Wiesbaden: Otto Harrassowitz, 1976), p. 29.

[22] Tonneson, 'The South China Sea in the Age of European Decline', pp. 22–4.

[23] Although France continued to hold some interests in the islands, with the First Indochina War beginning in earnest in late 1946, its concerns were soon directed elsewhere. That said, they did manage to occupy Pattle Island, laying the foundation for the peculiar situation that remained for much of the next 30 years whereby Chinese forces occupied the northeast Amphitrite group of the Paracels, while French/Vietnamese forces occupied the southwestern Crescent group of the Paracels.

24  M. Taylor Fravel, *Strong Borders, Secure Nation: Cooperation and Conflict in China's Territorial Disputes* (Princeton, NJ: Princeton University Press, 2008), p. 278.

25  This translates as: 'New Map Showing the Territorial Water and Continental Shelf Boundaries of Malaysia'. For a detailed exposition of Malaysia's claim and occupations, see: Asri Salleh, Che Hamdan Che Mohd Razali and Kamaruzaman Jusoff, 'Malaysia's Policy Towards its 1963–2008 Territorial Disputes', *Journal of Law and Conflict Resolution*, vol. 1, no. 5, October 2009, pp. 107–16.

26  Southeast Asia's first offshore well was drilled in 1957. In 1969, a report by the Economic Commission for Asia and the Far East suggested there was petroleum in the seas bordering China. See: Daniel J. Dzurek, 'The Spratly Islands Dispute: Who's On First?', IBRU *Maritime Briefing*, vol. 2, no. 1, 1996, p. 113.

27  Fravel, *Strong Borders, Secure Nation*, pp. 280–83.

28  Reliable statistics on the number of casualties are difficult to verify. China lost 18 sailors, and a Vietnamese White Paper from 1975 claimed 18 South Vietnamese personnel died and 43 were wounded (Vietnamese White Paper on the Hoang Sa and Truong Sa Islands, Vietnamese Ministry of Foreign Affairs, 1975). However, it is likely that more Vietnamese sailors died: Fravel mentions that 165 Vietnamese sailors were missing (Fravel, *Strong Borders, Secure Nation*, p. 272), and subsequent unofficial online Vietnamese-language sources have claimed 74 died, even providing names of the dead listed along with their vessel or unit (see, for instance, a report by the advocacy group Nguyen Thai Hoc Foundation: http://nguyenthaihocfoundation. org/lichsuVN/danhsach_74_tusi_ hoangsa.htm). Beijing also captured 48 people (all of whom were released within three weeks).

29  The features occupied were Spratly Island, Sin Cowe Island, Sand Cay, Namyit Island and Southwest Cay. Vietnam managed to take the Philippine-occupied Southwest Cay without bloodshed by sending its operation in while the Philippine personnel were on the nearby Northeast Cay for the commander's birthday party. There is some confusion over when Vietnam occupied Amboyna Cay. Salleh, Razali and Jusoff (2009) claim that it was occupied twice in 1956 and returned in 1973, but in the same paper also cite its year of occupation as 1975.

30  Mark J. Valencia, Jon M. Van Dyke and Noel A. Ludwig, *Sharing the Resources of the South China Sea* (Honolulu, HI: University of Hawaii Press, 1999), pp. 34–5.

31  See Salleh, Razali and Jusoff, 'Malaysia's Policy Towards its 1963–2008 Territorial Disputes', p. 113.

32  Cuarteron Reef, Fiery Cross Reef, Gaven Reef, Hughes Reef, Johnson South Reef and Subi Reef. It should be noted that Vietnam was to occupy Collins Reef (also known as Johnson North Reef) just 3km away from Johnson South Reef.

33  Namely Alexandra Bank, Alison Reef, Barque Canada Reef, Collins

Reef (Johnson North Reef), Cornwallis South Reef, Great Discovery Reef, East London Reef, Grainger Reef, Ladd Reef, Landsdowne Reef, Pearson Reef, Petley Reef, Pigeon Reef, Prince Consort Bank, Prince of Wales Bank, Rifleman Bank (a lighthouse at Bombay Castle, at the northern end of Rifleman Bank, was built in the early 1980s), Sin Cowe East Island, Vanguard Bank and West London Reef.

34 DJ Sta, 'China Builds more Spratly Outposts', *The Philippine Star*, 24 May 2011, http://www.philstar.com/headlines/688856/china-builds-more-spratly-outposts.

35 Ronald A. Rodriguez, 'Conduct Unbecoming in the South China Sea?', PacNet Number 22A, Pacific Forum CSIS, 21 May 2004, http://csis.org/files/media/csis/pubs/pac0422a.pdf.

36 ASEAN Declaration on the South China Sea, Manila, 22 July 1992.

37 While the joint submission by Vietnam and Malaysia and Vietnam's own unilateral submission did not mention the South China Sea islands per se, they laid claim to 200nm EEZs and continental shelf claims that extended to an equidistant line between Vietnam and Malaysia in the south and Vietnam and China in the north. This in turn instigated a series of notes and counter-notes from various states, including from China, Indonesia and the Philippines. Vietnam then responded with its own counter-note that affirmed its sovereignty over the Paracel and Spratly Islands.

38 That is, a civilian-crewed US Navy auxiliary vessel.

39 Marciel noted that 'starting in the summer of 2007, China told a number of US and foreign oil and gas firms to stop exploration work with Vietnamese partners in the South China Sea or face unspecified consequences in their business dealings with China'. Testimony of Deputy Assistant Secretary Scot Marciel, Subcommittee on East Asian and Pacific Affairs Committee on Foreign Relations, 15 July 2009, p. 4, accessed in January 2013 at http://vietnam.usembassy.gov/uploads/images/3VC0_Hwh5_paP5TLrjbLNg/MarcielTestimony090715p.pdf.

40 For a full list of the objections, see: Fravel, 'China's Strategy in the South China Sea', *Contemporary Southeast Asia*, vol. 33, no. 3, December 2011, p. 302.

41 Greg Torode, 'Beijing Pressure Intense in South China Sea Row', *South China Morning Post*, 23 September 2011, http://www.scmp.com/article/979876/beijing-pressure-intense-south-china-sea-row.

42 For a brief description of these incidents, see: Carlyle A. Thayer, 'Chinese Assertiveness in the South China Sea and Southeast Asian Responses', *Journal of Current Southeast Asian Affairs*, vol. 30, no. 2, 2011, pp. 77–104.

43 Senate Resolution 217. For full text, see: http://webb.senate.gov/newsroom/pressreleases/06-27-2011.cfm?renderforprint=1.

# CHAPTER TWO

# Beijing's multifaceted approaches

As the militarily most capable and economically most powerful of the claimant countries, China bears a particular burden of leadership in the management of sovereignty disputes in the South China Sea. As the previous chapter has charted, it is no coincidence that one consistent factor over the past few decades in explaining the shifting pattern between confrontation and détente in the South China Sea has been the nature of policies pursued by China. And as this chapter will make clear, present trends look set to ensure not only the continuing peculiar primacy of Chinese behaviour in shaping the tone for dispute management, but also the country's critical role in determining the broader strategic significance of these disputes for the emerging regional order. As the military modernisation of the PLA – and in particular the PLAN – continues, so the asymmetry between Chinese hard-power capabilities (and therefore options) and those of rival claimants is becoming starker. Meanwhile, Asia is continuing to become ever more economically integrated, with the overwhelming geoeconomic power of China lying at the heart of these expanding and overlapping networks of trade.

It is, then, reasonable to expect that these growing asymmetries of influence would, in and of themselves, have returned the South China Sea to the strategic centre-stage, regardless of any further actions on the part of Beijing. Moreover, as the previous chapter has highlighted, there have also been external factors contributing to renewed tensions which have been beyond Beijing's sole control (such as the May 2009 deadline for submissions for an extended continental shelf under UNCLOS). Nevertheless, Beijing has played its own active, if sometimes inadvertent, part in attracting attention to the disputes – to both their detail and the broader implications of their management for China's position within an evolving regional order.

## How 'assertive'?

Although the language of growing Chinese 'assertiveness' has now become embedded in the popular strategic vernacular, this chapter's particular focus on China should not be mistaken for an argument that assertiveness has been the sole prerogative of Beijing. Indeed, some have identified a Chinese policy of 'reactive assertiveness', whereby Beijing has not looked to force the pace on contentious issues but rather robustly to defend its standpoint when others have come encroaching. With reference, for example, to the stand-off between China and the Philippines at Scarborough Reef in 2012, British journalist and former Asia-Pacific editor of *Jane's Defence Weekly* Trefor Moss argued that China demonstrated 'non-confrontational assertiveness' through its assertive *re*actions, balanced with 'significant restraint'.[1]

Yet, whilst it is worthwhile mentioning this balancing perspective on action–reaction dynamics, the argument is ultimately a tricky one to sustain. China does not deserve credit simply for having more hard-power capabilities than a challenger and yet choosing not to deploy these.[2] This is the minimum 'restraint' one should expect in dispute management under international law. Whilst its preferred strategy of deploying paramilitary over military capabilities is worth noting – and indeed this chapter will go on to explore this in more detail – the observation of this trend does not equate to a refutation of assertiveness. Moreover, in the case of the 2012 stand-off at Scarborough Reef, China has ultimately succeeded in changing the status quo around the reef, thereby securing its objectives by smarter, but no less coercive means than the simple application of brute force, which would anyway likely have been counter-productive. More generally, whilst other less powerful actors may occasionally seek advantage in provocation, the moral burden of responsibility will always lie with the more powerful to appreciate the concerns driving the provocations of the less powerful.[3]

Others, however, have gone further even than Moss, questioning whether the adjective of 'assertiveness' is really fairly attributed to Chinese behaviour at all, noting, for example, that China's position on the South China Sea disputes has been broadly consistent since the late 1970s.[4] No new claims have been made by China either in terms of sovereignty or maritime rights since then. Meanwhile, China's May 2009 submission before UNCLOS simply reiterated a longstanding position and was precipitated by the need to defend against competing claims already submitted by others. Whilst the inclusion in this submission of the controversially expansive nine-dashed line map outlining Chinese claims may have been novel in as much as this was the People's Republic of China's first ever use of the map in official government documentation, the map itself dates back to the late 1940s.

Once again, the cautionary reminder of the backdrop in which other claimants are moving to shore up their respective claims is an important one. Certainly, the evidence cited in support of Chinese assertiveness can occasionally be a little shaky. Take, for example, the mooted elevation of Chinese sovereignty claims in the South China Sea to be – in official Chinese government language – a 'core interest'. Such a promotion would put Chinese interests in the sea on a par with issues including Taiwan and Tibet, on which China will not negotiate and in defence of which China stands ready to use force. Yet whilst media outlets, most notably China's state-controlled Xinhua News Agency, and even some Chinese diplomats have certainly referred to the South China Sea as part of China's 'core interests', the reality is that no senior Chinese leader has yet expressed this sentiment publicly.[5] And although it has been suggested that such claims have been made in private – including most notably by State Councillor Dai Bingguo in a May 2010 meeting with then Secretary of State Hillary Clinton during the US–China Strategic and Economic Dialogue – the precise accuracy and language of these claims remain unclear.[6] For example, a claim that the entire waters of the South China Sea constituted a 'core interest' is very different from a similar claim focused only on the sovereignty of contested islands. Whilst the former is certainly more provocative, the latter arguably falls within the boundaries of 'territorial integrity' – a long-established 'core interest' for China.

Nevertheless, there does appear to have been some upgrading of the terminology through which China frames its interests in the South China Sea. For example, the State Council's September 2011 White Paper on China's Peaceful Development listed for the first time 'sovereignty' as a 'core interest' alongside security, territorial integrity and national unity.[7] Although the document did not explicitly cite China's sovereignty claims in the South China Sea in these terms, the message to Beijing's neighbours and rival claimants was no less clear.

Therefore, whilst China may not yet actively be seeking the disruption of the status quo that the term 'assertiveness' might imply, the doggedness and dogma with which it pursues its consistent claims have nevertheless increased in recent years. Meanwhile, the gap between the rhetoric of cooperation and the reality of competition has become starker. Indeed, China's apparent commitment to diplomacy has not included a parallel enthusiasm for seeking conclusions to any negotiations. And whilst the talking continues, the facts on the ground are shifting – seemingly inexorably – in China's favour. As South China Sea scholar Ian Storey has noted, China's strategy has even been characterised in some parts of Southeast Asia as 'talk and take'.[8]

Ultimately, China has a difficult and perhaps impossible balance to achieve. It has to manage both the protection and prosecution of its sovereignty claims in the South China Sea in parallel with an ongoing diplomatic wooing of its neighbours in search of the peaceful periphery it seeks for its national and economic security. To make things more complicated, lessons from history combine with concerns about the future regional security implications of China's rising military and economic might to predispose these neighbours to be concerned about the impact of a rising China on their future autonomies of action. And even if these suspicions can be allayed and China's rhetorical rejections of hegemonic aspirations believed, China still has to deal with the overlapping dynamic of relations with a US which remains intent on retaining its role as the primary military power in Asia. As Cronin and Kaplan so neatly summarise, 'China may not want to control the entire region, but it clearly wants to be at the center of it'.[9] And at the centre of this region – both literally and figuratively – lies the South China Sea.

## Beijing's multi-layered approaches to the South China Sea

In recent years, Beijing has demonstrated an impressively comprehensive approach to the furthering of its interests in the South China Sea, bringing a range of levers to bear. Whilst questions over the coordination of these levers and the extent to which there is one overarching China strategy are considered later in this chapter, what is initially most noticeable is the sheer number of policy initiatives Beijing has developed across the spectrum of diplomatic, military/paramilitary, economic and administrative spheres in pursuit of its aims.

### Beijing's South China Sea diplomacy

With regard to the South China Sea disputes, diplomatic priority number one is to try to keep them off the agenda – whatever that agenda may be. In repeated visits over the past several years to Beijing to engage both officials and think tankers on these disputes, the message to the authors of this book was the same: there is no real problem other than one outsiders are artificially creating to pursue agendas of their own. There will be disagreements in some areas, but these are the business of those involved and will be better managed and more easily resolved from within. Such disputes do not belong on the agenda of the EAS, the ASEAN Regional Forum, or even the ASEAN summit. Indeed, as the *People's Daily* put it when discussing preparations for the 20th ASEAN summit in 2012, 'some Western media and a few countries' actions of distorting the theme of the ASEAN Summit, deliberately exaggerating the South China Sea issue, creating confrontation between China and the ASEAN ... are actually severe disturbances for promoting the integration process of the ASEAN ... Some large external countries intend to seize the dominance of the region and deliberately damage the China-ASEAN relations.'[10] As the same newspaper again reminded its readers just a few months later, 'the South China Sea is currently calm and peaceful'.[11]

Officials are similarly anxious to reassure. In the wake of Chinese harassment of Philippine and Vietnamese survey vessels, at the June 2011 Shangri-La Dialogue, Chinese Defence Minister Liang Guanglie outlined the 'stable' situation in the sea, reminding delegates of China's commitment to 'peace and stability' in the region.[12] Specific points of concern are regularly dismissed in Beijing with a flurry of finger-pointing at the bigger picture of economic cooperation. As tensions between China and the Philippines heightened in early 2012 around Scarborough Reef, the Chinese ambassador to the Philippines quoted from a Chinese poem to describe the bigger picture of bilateral relations: 'I do not fear that the flowing clouds may block my vision, for where I stand is the top of the mountain'.[13]

Where problems over competing sovereignty claims are recognised by Beijing, such acknowledgement does not extend to contested claims over the Paracels. Even bilateral attempts at dialogue by rival claimant Vietnam are repeatedly rebuffed by China, which has enjoyed sole control there since seizing the remaining islands in 1974. As one senior Chinese South China Sea academic expert commented, 'There is no dispute in the Paracels. Therefore we do not discuss it.'[14] Meanwhile, with regard to the Spratlys, where rival claims are at least acknowledged if not recognised, Beijing insists that the appropriate forum for discussions is firmly bilateral rather than multilateral. For example, whilst China's first ambassador to ASEAN, Xue Hanqin, may have been appointed in what Beijing styled a 'new era' of Sino-ASEAN relations, she remained resolute that this new goodwill did not mean that Beijing was ready to discuss claims with anyone but the claimants themselves, and then only bilaterally.[15]

By seeking to keep discussions over disputes within a series of bilateral frameworks, Beijing aims to strengthen its position through the age-old tactic of 'divide and rule'. Following the 2002 signing of the ASEAN–China DoC, China worked hard to keep the disputes from returning to the multilateral agenda. The wider the multilateral body, the harder China fought. And for many years it largely succeeded, for example keeping the South China Sea off the agenda of the ASEAN Regional Forum until July 2010, when ASEAN claimants joined eight other countries to raise common concern about recent Chinese actions in the sea. Even the ASEAN summit itself is repeatedly declared by Beijing as 'not the proper occasion' for discussions on the South China Sea.[16]

When China does accede to multilateral negotiations, therefore, it tends to be as a tactical retreat under pressure. The apparent aim is to give multilateral negotiations with ASEAN – the smallest of the possible relevant multilateral forums – sufficient momentum as to undermine the grounds for broader external 'interference', chiefly in the form of US engagement on the issue. For example, the 'Guidelines' of July 2011 came about in part as a tactical counter to growing US engagement through 2009–2010. With minimal concessions made by any of the protagonists over and above commitments already signed under the DoC almost a decade earlier, for Beijing this appeared to be more about cutting away at the pretext offered by the South China Sea for US regional alliance-building, than it was a serious attempt to progress from the declaration to a more substantive and legally binding code.[17] (Indeed, in a further demonstration of its preference for bilateral negotiations, a few months later China also concluded a separate agreement with Vietnam which was arguably more substantial in establishing a set of basic principles for resolving maritime disputes under international law.)[18]

Given the apparent effectiveness of this stick of US engagement, it is perhaps unsurprising that ASEAN nations are repeatedly warned by China against involving the US in these disputes. In 2010, Chinese Ambassador to the Philippines Liu Juanchao publicly warned his hosts that any attempts to involve a third party in bilateral sovereignty disputes between China and the Philippines would result in a 'situation that neither country would like to see'.[19] As tensions rose again in 2012, another former Chinese ambassador to the Philippines joined in the fray: 'Americans should not involve themselves in the South China Sea issue … it would be wise for the nations concerned in this region, including the Philippines that we better not to introduce the Americans into the troubled waters … because that would make the issue more complicated.'[20]

Finally, in a further attempt to reduce the US influence on the debate and isolate weaker claimants, in 2012 China adopted the interesting tactic of highlighting US official statements of neutrality with regard to the substance of the sovereignty disputes. The underlying point was clear: the likes of Vietnam or the Philippines cannot risk escalation without US support, and such support is by no means guaranteed.

Meanwhile, China seeks to make the most of its influence in Southeast Asia to dilute and damage the already-problematic prospects for a united ASEAN front on these disputes. When, in July 2012, the ASEAN foreign ministers meeting failed for the first time in their history to issue a joint communiqué, with participants unable to agree on a text that included mention of the South China Sea, the fact that China's close ally Cambodia was hosting the summit and proved the major obstruction to inclusion of a mention of the sea was a reminder of the influence Beijing can exercise over a multilateral body of which it is not even a member. As attention following the summit focused on this influence, and in a way that threatened to be potentially counter-productive to Chinese interests, Chinese regional diplomacy was brought back to the forefront, with Foreign Minister Yang Jiechi deployed to shore up regional relations through a tour that focused on Indonesia, Malaysia and Brunei, whilst conveniently excluding the more problematic Vietnam and the Philippines.

## Beijing's military advances in the South China Sea

Although China's influence in the region is more complex and far reaching than a simple focus on its increasing hard-power capabilities might suggest, the rapid pace and nature of Chinese military modernisation nevertheless provides an important undercurrent to concerns over the future of the South China Sea. Whilst the key driver for the PLA's modernisation remains Taiwan, the PLAN in particular has been taking on a higher profile in the defence of other national interests, including the protection of sea lines of communication and the prosecution of sovereignty disputes in the South and East China Seas.

The PLAN has witnessed impressive growth and investment since the early 1990s, when then Chinese President Jiang Zemin began to prioritise naval development in what had traditionally been a land-centric military. This reflected the shift in China's strategic position: it no longer feared an invasion of massed forces and felt confident that it could rebuff most of its neighbours in conventional warfare. Hence, its attention could begin to focus on interests beyond its coastline to its near seas and expanding overseas interests.

The result has been a wholesale modernisation of the navy, with new destroyers, frigates, corvettes, amphibious assault vessels, fast-attack craft, submarines and even an aircraft-carrier programme. Three decades of nearly continuous double-digit defence-spending growth has allowed Beijing to transform its navy from the one that was reliant on outdated vessels and equipment in the 1980s (including early Cold War-era destroyer and frigate designs) and submarines that were modelled on Second World War-era Soviet and German technology.[21] Various improvements have resulted from this increase in defence spending, and capable anti-ship missiles and radar technologies are now routinely fitted on Chinese vessels. This has meant that the PLAN, while still inferior in technology and probably training to the leading regional navies of Japan and South Korea, is now several leagues ahead of any of the Southeast Asian navies with which it competes for territory in the South China Sea.

Its growth in capabilities has also been matched by a shift in geographical focus: traditionally the dominant fleet in China's tri-fleet service has been the East Sea Fleet, which is the primary agent tasked with any Taiwan contingency. Although this remains the case, as evidenced by the delivery from Russia of *Sovremenny*-class destroyers and *Kilo*-class submarines to the East Sea Fleet in the mid-2000s, the South Sea Fleet has been catching up fast. The first two Type 052C destroyers – currently the most advanced and powerful vessels in the Chinese navy – were delivered to the South Sea Fleet in 2004 and 2005. In fact, five of the seven indigenous modern destroyers China has developed in the last ten years are based with this fleet, which has also received the first Type 071 amphibious assault vessels.[22] In the early 2000s, the South Sea Fleet also saw the construction of the most significant naval base, the Yulin base, in China in decades. On the South China Sea coastline, near Sanya on Hainan Island, the base now boasts an underground submarine base, four piers and a wharf large enough to replenish an aircraft carrier. Although some of its assets (such as the Type 094 ballistic missile submarine) are more strategic than tactical, and therefore of little utility in the South China Sea, the base itself is both an indication of the geographical shift witnessed by the PLAN in recent years and of the growing strategic importance of the sea itself.

Control of the Paracel Islands to the immediate south of Hainan is therefore useful in ensuring that no hostile power retains territory situated in the approach to Yulin. Meanwhile, further south still, control if not sovereignty over the Spratlys enables the monitoring of traffic through the sea, including the use of some intelligence-gathering capabilities, and the theoretical housing of anti-ship missiles that could threaten larger vessels transiting through the area. Should China wish to deploy its carrier to the Indian Ocean, therefore, control over the South China Sea is a prerequisite for its safe transit.

This strategic importance is reflected in the fact that the South China Sea potentially offers one of the few sanctuaries for China's naval assets against attack, while also promising the access to the open seas required by larger vessels and submarines through the Luzon Strait. Currently, China fears an encirclement to its east by South Korea, Japan and Taiwan, all strong US allies and all capable of denying access to the open ocean to some extent. The Luzon Strait between the Philippines and Taiwan and the Miyako Strait through Japan's Okinawa islands represent the best forms of transport to the Pacific Ocean for the PLAN, and the latter sails closer to the effective anti-ship missiles, submarines and anti-submarine warfare combatants of a traditional rival. China is, for the first time, now developing a survivable, continuous-at-sea deterrence through its Type 094 SSBNs and JL-2 submarine-launched ballistic missile (the first-generation JL-1 missile had a range too short to be globally relevant and was only deployed on one Type 092 submarine, ensuring that it could not be deployed continuously, a policy that requires at least three and preferably four boats). However, such submarines require access to the open seas as they patrol for several months at various depths to avoid detection and create a constant deterrent. To assure this access, therefore, China requires at least the ability to counter interference from other naval powers potentially interested in limiting this access, and ideally control over the South China Sea as a whole.[23]

An increase in the tempo, scale and ambition of Chinese military exercises provides regular reminders, in particular to China's Southeast Asian neighbours, of the country's growing naval capabilities. For example, in July 2010, the South Sea Fleet hosted a large-scale, live-ammunition exercise in the South China Sea joined by all three fleets. In November 2010, another South Sea Fleet exercise played out an amphibious landing on a beach head involving an impressive array of equipment including submarine chasers, amphibious armoured vehicles, landing craft and assault boats.[24] In January 2013, a PLA exercise simulated raids by *Hong*-6 bombers attacking a harbour in an open sea area more than 1,000km away from Zhanjiang naval base in Guangdong after having avoided enemy radar and electromagnetic interference.[25] The concern for the US and its allies is obvious: slowly but surely China is amassing the capabilities to dominate the South China Sea.

China's military build-up should not, therefore, be viewed simply in comparison to the weaker states of Southeast Asia. Cognisant of its potential rivalry with the US, and perhaps US allies such as Japan, the PLAN is also developing a variety of asymmetric capabilities that the Pentagon has described in aggregate as anti-area/access denial (A2AD) capabilities. In fact, these A2AD capabilities are the primary reason for the shift in the US position in Asia, with US forces increasingly dispersed over a number of bases in order to complicate Chinese planning, intelligence and reactions to any task group that could now utilise multiple lines of approach.[26] Capabilities such as anti-satellite weapons, 'carrier-killer' anti-ship ballistic missiles, information-warfare capabilities and fast-attack craft armed with nothing but anti-ship missiles and intended to harry larger vessels in the littorals, now form the backbone of China's military strategy in any contingency with a superior navy.

However, Beijing's strategy in the South China Sea is smarter than a naked showcasing of the obvious improvements in its hard-power capabilities. While the PLA appears to take primacy in defending contested territory where China already has control, the maritime law-enforcement agencies appear to take on the role of asserting Chinese maritime rights stemming from territorial claims made but not yet necessarily fully controlled.[27] Thus, when it comes to the South China Sea, the PLAN is kept firmly and deliberately in the background, whilst these maritime constabulary agencies are given centre-stage. The China Maritime Police, the Maritime Safety Administration, the Fisheries Law Enforcement Command, the General Administration of Customs and China Marine Surveillance (CMS) are the front-line actors in China's enforcement of its sovereignty and maritime claims. In particular, the vessels of the Fisheries Law Enforcement Command and CMS are regularly to be found patrolling the South China Sea or deployed in support of Chinese fishermen in the region.[28]

The use of these maritime paramilitaries, rather than the PLAN, in enforcing sovereignty and confronting neighbours' fishing vessels carries a number of benefits for China.[29] Firstly, maritime paramilitary vessels may unnerve rivals but are perceived as less confrontational than naval vessels. Although the argument that this strategy is a sign of Chinese 'restraint' falls a little flat when one considers that the full force of the PLAN stands so obviously behind these paramilitary vessels, their deployment will not cause alarm to the same extent as a military flotilla bristling with anti-ship missiles and rapid-fire guns. In turn, this means that the intended target will be less likely to react rashly in the face of these unarmed vessels. Secondly, maritime paramilitary activities are generally more containable and less escalatory than those of navies. There is a subtle difference here between the threat perception of the first benefit, which is largely in the mind of the rival power, and the capabilities offered in the second benefit. Paramilitaries both allow a demilitarisation of potentially fraught disagreements whilst also adding another rung to the bottom of the ladder of escalatory options available, whereby the unarmed vessel can be deployed first and, if necessary, a military vessel later. Thirdly, there is no interpretation of UNCLOS that would suggest a restriction to the activities of civilian vessels, even state-owned non-military vessels, in the 200nm EEZ, in contrast to China's objection to military surveillance activities by the US in its own EEZ. This therefore avoids any legal complexities in its own position toward foreign military surveillance activities. Lastly, the use of a paramilitary can also send a subliminal message: these are already our waters and we don't need to defend them with naval assets. Much like a police car will only be able to patrol a village on land in undisputed sovereign territory, so the maritime paramilitaries suggest that their constabulary activities are feasible precisely because this is already sovereign territory.

The benefits to the deployment of these maritime law enforcement agencies mean that they are patrolling both with greater regularity and assertiveness. According to China's own reporting, the South Sea Fleet of the CMS force conducted nearly three times as many missions in 2011 as it did in 2008.[30] In order to fulfil this growing role, the force has been significantly bolstered in recent years. In 2010, officials claimed that 36 more vessels would be added to the fleet in coming years – comprising seven 1,500-tonne, 15 1,000-tonne and 14 600-tonne vessels.[31] The CMS's responsibilities now extend far beyond the surveillance role for which it was first created in 1998. This is well illustrated by that fact that, in early 2012, Beijing deployed two CMS ships, the *Zhonggou Haijian 75* and *Zhonggou Haijian 84*, to prevent the arrest by the Philippines of Chinese fishermen accused of illegal fishing in the Scarborough Reef.[32]

Indeed, China's management of its stand-off with the Philippines at Scarborough Reef in 2012 might yet be the clearest example of a developing strategy; fishermen are encouraged to press Chinese territorial claims, whilst Chinese paramilitary stand ready to come to their aid in the event of problems. The disputed area is in turn overwhelmed by an array of Chinese ships, giving the rival claimant the unattractive policy option of fight or flight.

At least for the moment then, the presence of China's military forces, except by implication, is judged unnecessary. Instead patience, perseverance and force of presence is used to wear a rival down – a task made easier in the 2012 stand-off at Scarborough Reef by ASEAN's failure substantively to support the Philippines, following their initial deployment of a flag ship to arrest Chinese fishermen, which was interpreted in some quarters as recklessly escalatory.

However, where required, the PLA can move from the background to the foreground, often still in close coordination with commercial and paramilitary actors. Such moves are more likely to be focused on certain aspects of the US presence in the South China Sea than on rival island claimants. More aggressive displays of Chinese power are therefore reserved for acts which seem, from Beijing's perspective, more hostile and where Beijing sees itself as having limited alternative options for protest.[33] This means that 'non-peaceful activities' by the US, including military reconnaissance, are met at least by a reminder (and occasionally more) of China's ability to deploy non-peaceful countermeasures. This tactic stretches back to the early 2000s, when the PLA began aggressive interceptions of US reconnaissance flights off the coast of China, including the EP-3 incident of 2001.[34] Later that decade, US Navy ships conducting similar activities also began to attract similar harassment, including most notoriously the USNS *Impeccable* in March 2009, as it sailed 75 miles south of Hainan. This incident saw the combined deployment of one PLAN ocean-surveillance ship with one patrol vessel from the Fisheries Law Enforcement Command, one patrol vessel from CMS and two fishing trawlers.

From Beijing's perspective, the escalation to this more aggressive counteraction of US activities, which it interprets as being hostile to Chinese interests, is a reasonable one. Moreover, growing US interest in Chinese military capabilities means that it is highly likely that such perceived 'provocations' on the part of the US have been occurring more regularly over the past decade, and at a time when Chinese military capabilities at the least to protest these aggravations have similarly been increasing. It is therefore no surprise that 'incidents at sea' are occurring. The immediate problem is how to regulate such behaviour to ensure that the dangers inherent in these challenges are limited, with rules of acceptable behaviours codified and responses agreed, and with the aim of managing the consequences of any challenge which did result in a more serious 'incident'.

## Beijing's economic leverage

A burgeoning military is not the only lever that Beijing has to pull when dealing with the South China Sea disputes and its relations with Southeast Asia. The country's economic rise and its meteoric growth in trade with the region mean China can also utilise its extensive economic influence in its diplomacy.

In 2011, China's trade with ASEAN countries was US$400 billion, and rising. Although there continue to be some problems in its actual functioning, the China–ASEAN region now hosts the world's largest free-trade agreement, covering a market containing some 1.9bn people and a trade volume upwards of US$4.5 trillion.[35] Whilst some of these interactions are a cause of tension – for example with regard to concerns over the valuation of the yuan or Chinese dumping practices – they generally serve as a driver for closer cooperation. Beijing is even looking to use its deep pockets to cultivate closer regional ties in the domain of maritime security, establishing, for example, in November 2011 a China–ASEAN Maritime Cooperation Fund backed by 3bn yuan (approximately US$475m) as well as hosting workshops on issues such as freedom of navigation. Although there is little sign that this will have a direct practical effect – the fund was only formally announced by ASEAN in October 2012 and no events had been held by then – its creation is a sign of Beijing's interest in investment as a means of influence in Southeast Asia. Meanwhile, China has developed a parallel role in the development of Southeast Asian economies as one of the key dispensers of aid in the region.

Whilst regional security concerns show no sign of holding up closer economic integration, increasing economic interactions across the region likewise show little sign of defusing underlying tensions, at least between rival claimants. For example, China doubled its foreign investment in the Philippines in 2010, whilst bilateral trade increased by 35%.[36] This has not stopped the Philippines moving towards a closer security partnership with the US, at least in the short term. Many in Southeast Asia understand that their own economic development continues in part on the coat tails of China's rise, but they are also concerned to insure in security terms against the increasingly apparent economic leverage which China is developing across the region.

Moreover, China's track record appears to justify concerns that it could deploy its economic leverage for political ends in the South China Sea. For example, it demonstrated both capability and intent in the East China Sea through an (officially unconfirmed) embargo on the export of rare earth minerals to Japan in September 2010 following Japan's detention of a Chinese captain whose fishing trawler had rammed two Japan Coast Guard vessels near the disputed Senkaku/Diaoyu Islands. Meanwhile, in 2012, China exhibited a similar willingness to use economic leverage for political ends in Southeast Asia. In the midst of the stand-off between China and the Philippines at Scarborough Reef, Beijing suddenly imposed restrictions on the import of Philippine bananas, allegedly for health reasons.[37] The target of these restrictions was well chosen; bananas are the Philippines' second-biggest agricultural export. Early on in the dispute, the executive director of the Philippine Banana Growers and Exports Association estimated that as many as 200,000 people in Mindanao – the centre of the Philippine banana business – stood to lose their livelihood should curbs on imports continue.[38] Inspection of other imported fruit from the Philippines was also slowed down. Meanwhile, trips to the Philippines by Chinese tour groups – the fastest growing source of foreign tourists for the Philippines – were cancelled due to security concerns after a travel advisory warning was issued by Beijing following a small anti-China protest in Manila.

This follows a broader pattern whereby trade flows and the Chinese foreign-policy agenda can be closely interlinked. This is in part because of its authoritarian political system and the significant role that the state continues to play in the economy, as it allows trade flows to be clearly utilised as a tool of foreign policy – whether to cultivate a particular partner or punish a particular foe.[39]

The impact of China's economic leverage also provides an important backdrop to the differing attitudes of non-claimant members of ASEAN towards the management of South China Sea disputes. As the next chapter will go on to explore, ASEAN unity on the issue of the management of these disputes has long been open to doubt. All indications are that differing degrees of economic patronage on the part of Beijing are playing an important role in further weakening the ground for a substantive ASEAN alliance on this issue.

*Whose hydrocarbons?*
Whilst Beijing continues in theory to propound former Chinese leader Deng Xiaoping's proposed solution for maritime disputes of putting claims of sovereignty to one side in favour of concentrating on joint development, the reality is that the presence of hydrocarbons in the South China Sea appears not so much to unite claimants but to divide them. Moreover, growing domestic demand for energy resources along with increasing dependencies on foreign and distant sources of supply – with the associated vulnerabilities this brings – is sharpening the competition in this area. In 2009 China, for example, became the world's second-largest consumer of oil, and its consumption is expected to double by 2030. Meanwhile, its oil reserve to production ratio has dropped to under ten years. The additional anticipated production from the South China Sea is therefore considered capable of potentially doubling Chinese reserves.[40]

Estimates of energy resources in the South China Sea vary considerably, but upper estimates tend to come from Chinese sources. On the sidelines of the 18th Party Congress in November 2012, Wang Yilin, head of China's biggest offshore oil and gas company, the China National Offshore Oil Corporation (CNOOC), suggested that the sea could hold 17bn tonnes of oil and 498tr cubic feet of natural gas.[41] Whilst only a fraction of these reserves are likely to prove economically viable to exploit, even the dream that the sea could prove a 'second Persian Gulf' is inevitably increasing the stakes surrounding these sovereignty disputes.[42]

Perhaps understandably, the type of 'joint development' of resources envisaged by Beijing would include a role for China. To that end, it has been a dissenting observer of joint development in the South China Sea both between Southeast Asian countries, and more often, Southeast Asian countries and their international partners. For example, from 2006–07, China issued 18 diplomatic objections to foreign oil companies involved in exploration and development projects with Vietnam.[43] As the previous chapter charted, such diplomatic protests have, in recent years, evolved into more direct action, including the intimidation of international oil companies and the engagement of paramilitary activity against survey ships representing these offending interests. Yet the vehemence of these responses has been inconsistent and unpredictable, likely deliberately so as Beijing carefully calibrates how hard and fast it can push its partners, and rivals, in the region. Therefore whilst some Vietnamese and Philippine vessels have suffered harassment when operating in disputed waters, others have been allowed to operate without confrontation.[44]

China has also begun opening up new blocks in the South China Sea to oil and gas tenders, and these have been increasingly controversial. For example, in June 2012, the China National Offshore Oil Company announced nine new blocks open to foreign investment located squarely within disputed waters, with the western edge of some blocks appearing to lie under 80nm from Vietnam's coast and, therefore, well within Vietnam's claimed EEZ.[45] Moreover, the offer includes large parts of blocks already leased by Vietnam to major oil companies, including the US's ExxonMobil and Russia's Gazprom.[46] Although China has yet to grant any licences to explore the blocks, the deliberate overlapping geography could act as a deterrent to continued overseas investment in blocks leased by Vietnam.

As explorations continue, as more surveys prove successful and as more technologies for deep-water exploitation emerge, it is reasonable to foresee more incidents at sea resulting from the competition for hydrocarbons, impacting not just those involved in hydrocarbon exploration and exploitation, but potentially those involved in the shipping industry more generally, including secondary industries such as maritime insurance.[47] Indeed, the commissioning of the first deep-water rig for Chinese state-owned oil firm CNOOC in 2012 (CNOOC 981 CK) offered a further indication of Beijing's interest in pushing the boundaries of exploration in the South China Sea. Upon its launch, in a blatant admission of the reasoning supporting this investment, CNOOC Chairman Wang Yilin declared, 'large-scale deep-water rigs are our mobile national territory and a strategic weapon'.[48]

*Whose fish stocks?*
Despite obvious common interests in the sustainable management of fish stocks in the South China Sea, which provide for up to 10% of the global catch used for human consumption, these resources have likewise proved more a source of regional tension than cooperation. Again China is not alone in its support of fishermen as the 'front-line' in regular and repeated assertions of national sovereignty. Nevertheless, at times commentators have even advocated a militarisation of China's fishing fleet. In June 2012, He Jianbin, chief of the state-run Baosha Fishing Corporation, stated 'if we put 5,000 Chinese fishing boats in the South China Sea, there will be

10,000 fishermen. And if we make all of them militiamen, give them weapons, we will have a military force stronger than all the combined forces of the countries in the South China Sea.'[49]

China has the world's largest fishing fleet and, in part because of its growing numbers and capabilities, it has arguably been the most visible of claimants in deploying its fleet in support of its presence in the sea's disputed areas. It is also perhaps the most organised in terms of its approach. For example, in July 2012, in one of the largest fishing expeditions in the history of Hainan province, 29 fishing boats and one 3,000-tonne supply vessel set sail for the Spratly Islands for a two-day fishing operation off Johnson North/South Reef. In an indication of the level of planning and organisation supporting this deployment to disputed waters, the fleet had a commander, three deputy commanders, and a control team to coordinate the activities of the sub-teams whilst fishing.[50]

Meanwhile, vessels from China's Fisheries Law Enforcement Command are also regularly deployed to escort Chinese fishing boats operating in disputed waters. These stand ready to provide aid and protect fishermen rights in the event of a challenge, whilst providing a visible reminder of Chinese claims of jurisdiction over the waters in question. China's fleet plays a critical role in China's national food security and regional economic development, as it aims to meet growing domestic demand while resources deplete and the marine environment in its inshore waters degrades.[51] Under these circumstances, as Chinese fishing vessels become more capable of operating further out to sea, including in disputed waters, and as their ventures are supported by more patrol boats, so a greater incidence of confrontations becomes, to some extent, inevitable. For example, enforcement is taken particularly seriously by the Chinese around the Paracels, leading to repeated and occasionally deadly clashes with Vietnamese fishing boats in particular. Aside from the usual 'expulsions' from the area, fishermen are also detained and boats seized. Release fees can be extortionate. When China detained two Vietnamese fishing boats and 21 crew members in the Paracels in March 2012, it demanded 70,000 yuan (US$11,000) for their release.

Since June 1999, China has imposed a unilateral fishing ban in the northern part of the South China Sea during the summer months, aimed at replenishing vital but shrinking fish stocks. Originally only applied to Chinese vessels, the length of the ban was increased in 2009, and its link to claims of Chinese sovereignty made more explicit.[52] Maritime security patrols aimed at enforcing the ban have been stepped up and foreign vessels – largely Vietnamese by nature of the ban's geography – have also been targeted. In 2012, the Philippines announced its first fishing ban amid the stand-off over Scarborough Reef, which coincided exactly with the Chinese ban.

**Beijing's administrative diplomacy**
Fishing bans and constabulary support for fishermen encourage the perception that the resources in the sea are Beijing's to administer, and thus suggest a degree of sovereignty over them. Similarly, a further tactic on the part of Beijing for projecting its claims in the South China Sea has been the gradual development of domestic law and international submissions aimed at codifying these claims. Some of these submissions and laws have mainly involved simply aligning established Chinese claims with provisions under UNCLOS. For example, in 1992, the 'Law of the People's Republic of China on the Territorial Sea and contiguous zone' reaffirmed Chinese sovereignty over the Paracels and the Spratlys, the Pratas Islands, Macclesfield Bank and Scarborough Reef (amongst others), claiming the accompanying 12nm territorial seas and adjacent contiguous

zones. Based on this legislation, four years later the country submitted its baselines to the UN, notably excluding the Spratly and Senkaku/Diaoyu Islands and Taiwan (but including the Paracels, suggesting Chinese desire to cement its control of, and therefore theoretical sovereignty over, the islands). In 1998 the 'Law on the Exclusive Economic Zone and Continental Shelf' claimed Chinese jurisdiction over an EEZ of 200nm out from Chinese territory, along with continental shelf rights. At times, international or domestic law has been used in a clear attempt to pressure other states diplomatically, or to build a stronger legal case. For example, in September 2012 amid an intense row with Japan in the East China Sea over the latter's purchase of three of the disputed Senkaku/Diaoyu Islands from a Japanese civilian, China updated its baselines, including the islands for the first time.

However, other domestic legal developments have been significantly more contentious. For example, in November 2007, rumours surfaced that China was preparing to upgrade the administrative status of the islands claimed from county level to prefecture level, creating a new city named Sansha to manage the island chains and their surrounding waters from its local government base on Woody Island in the Paracels.[53] Protestors quickly rallied on the streets of Hanoi, and the test balloon was duly lowered for several years. Indeed, no official announcement of this move was made until June 2012, when it was conveniently scripted in some quarters as a response to a new law passed by Vietnam's National Assembly which clearly defined its sovereignty as including the disputed Spratly and Paracel archipelagos.[54] While Chinese concerns at the move by Vietnam were understandable, the claim that the upgrading of Sansha was simply a counter-move was less credible. The plans were already in place; Vietnam simply provided the pretext for the go-ahead.

However, China is not the only country to utilise such administrative diplomacy: the Philippines designated its claimed Spratly Islands to be part of Palawan province in 1972; and Vietnam has placed the Spratlys under the administration of Khanh Hoa province, and the Paracels under Da Nanh province (although they were previously under the Phuoc Tuy and Quang Nam provinces).

Nonetheless, China's Sansha announcement represented a noteworthy upgrade in administration, preparing the way for more officials to be sent to the islands for 'administrative purposes' and with more jurisdictional power. A month later it was announced that a military garrison would be formed in the city. Although this is not expected to lead to a significant increase in military deployments, it does represent a political and administrative reorganisation of the current deployment, with the garrison now subordinate to the Hainan Military Command, rather than being directly under the South Sea Fleet. Ostensibly defensive and essentially designed to improve coordination between the military and administrative divisions within the South China Sea, the basis for the decision appears to be political rather than military. Nevertheless, the militaristic overtones are clear, with the city's top priority being to safeguard Chinese sovereignty over the disputed islands and waters.[55]

This move towards a more assertive tenor in China's pursuit of its South China Sea claims was further reinforced in November 2012, when the Hainanese People's Congress passed a resolution stating that, from January 2013, the border police would stop and search vessels in Chinese waters that were deemed to be breaking Chinese law. It specified the disputed South China Sea islands as an area where more patrols were needed to administer 'Chinese waters'. It is not clear to what extent this resolution will have practical consequences; the regulations only applied to the claimed 12nm sovereign territory around China's coastline and islands under Hainan's administration. While this could theoretically lead to harassment of shipping around the South China Sea islands, in reality few international shipping companies travel that close to the shallow waters near the islands and the Hainanese border police have limited seagoing capabilities.[56] Nevertheless, this was a significant diplomatic announcement and reflective of China's attempts to clarify its administration of the region.

Other moves have accompanied and complimented the developments outlined above. In October 2012, China's State Oceanic Administration was reported to have requested provincial authorities to conduct an island census by April 2013, to include the naming of previously nameless features. Focused not just on the South China Sea, but designed to support Chinese sovereignty claims in China's entire maritime periphery, this was reported as involving the naming of a further 1,664 features by August 2013.[57] In December 2012, a diplomatic storm also arose over Beijing's new e-passports, showing a map of Chinese territory on page eight which included its South China Sea claims (as well as Himalayan land under dispute with India). Protests quickly followed, with Vietnam and the Philippines refusing to issue visas for these new passports, anxious not to do anything that could imply acceptance of China's claims.[58] The Indonesian foreign minister labelled the move 'counterproductive' for regional relations, noting, 'We perceive the Chinese move as disingenuous, like testing the water, to see its neighbours' reactions'.[59] Meanwhile, Beijing and local authorities have also been taking steps to encourage more Chinese travel to the islands, even if only as visitors.[60] Again, China is not alone in this endeavour: Vietnam has already developed a tourism route to the Spratly Islands in a bid to normalise the transportation of

Vietnamese citizens to the area, while Malaysia has promoted disputed features such as Louisa Reef and the Luconia Shoals as prime diving spots. In China's case, an earlier example can be found, in January 2010, when China's State Council issued guidelines on developing tourism in Hainan province, which included the Paracels. Plans for tourism promotion strategies have since been advanced by the Hainan Tourism Development Commission in coordination with the National Tourism Administration. With no civilian airlines or cruise boats currently connecting the islands to other parts of China, travel is difficult at present. But efforts are reportedly under-way to change this. One Chinese cruise operator, the Hainan Strait Shipping company, claims already to have been granted a licence to operate the Haikou–Sanya–Northern Paracels route.[61] As former deputy director of the National Tourism Administration and Chinese People's Political Consultative Conference (CPPCC) member Zhang Xiqin has admitted, the promotion of tourism to the islands is 'not simply an exploration of travel resources, it's more about safeguarding sovereignty over these islands ... Allow our citizens to step on the Islands and they will have a stronger feeling that the Islands are indispensable parts of China.'[62]

Such comments also raise interesting questions over the degree to which Beijing deliberately cultivates and deploys popular nationalism as a lever in the projection of its sover-eignty claims, as opposed to the degree to which these claims are themselves driven by popular nationalism. As will become clear when this subject is addressed in greater detail later in this chapter, whilst popular nationalism grows more organi-cally when news reports of 'provocations' by other claimants surface, Beijing would appear at times to be at the very least complicit in a continuing cultivation of underlying nationalism with regard to its island claims.

## The domestic challenges of Beijing's South China Sea strategies

This chapter has highlighted the considerable range of levers available to Beijing in the prosecution of its South China Sea claims, across diplomatic, military, economic and administrative fields. However, it is important to note that there are also impediments to Beijing's precise control of these levers as it seeks to calibrate how assertive to be, where and when in the promotion of its interests in the South China Sea.

### The challenge of bureaucratic and policy coordination

The number of bureaucratic institutions involved in the management of China's South China Sea interests, at both a central and regional level, is certainly dazzling. Problems of coordination between these assorted bodies are repeatedly cited as a source of Chinese policy weakness. As M. Taylor Fravel has commented, 'in the past ten years, the number of actors with the ability to influence Chinese policy in maritime affairs has grown much faster than the ability of the state to regulate and coordinate them'.[63] Indeed the array of actors involved and their respective remits are the subject of a detailed report by International Crisis Group. It uses the old Chinese saying of 'nine dragons stirring up the sea' to highlight the danger that this proliferation of agencies, with their competing agendas and budgets, is beginning itself to drive Chinese policy interests, as opposed to simply serving and executing those interests.[64]

This danger is illustrated by the overlapping mandates and responsibilities of China's five central maritime law-enforcement agencies:

- The China Coast Guard, whose main responsibility is crime-fighting, belongs to the Public Security Ministry.
- The Maritime Safety Administration is responsible amongst other things for the inspection of ships and

vessel traffic control, and comes under the Transport
Ministry.

- The Fisheries Law Enforcement Command, which has
fewer men than the China Coast Guard but some larger
vessels, oversees all fishery activities and falls under the
Agriculture Ministry.

- China Marine Surveillance, which sits under the auspices
of the State Oceanographic Administration and is the ultimate responsibility of the Land and Resources Ministry,
is charged with protecting the environment (excluding
fish resources), conducting marine surveys and enforcing the law of the EEZ.

- The General Administration of Customs focuses on
collecting customs duties and preventing smuggling.

Of course, each of these five agencies also has its own
paramilitary units, equipped with increasingly capable and
significant vessels, including decommissioned navy frigates.[65]
Meanwhile, other, smaller agencies, including provincial
governments and local police and customs, also field patrol
boats and surveillance vessels.

Proposals have been floated to streamline responsibilities, for
example, by creating a single coast guard unit, similar to that
operated by Japan, the US or Russia.[66] But for the moment the
respective interests behind those groups which would need
to be involved (including the Ministry of Public Security, the
State Oceanographic Administration and the Fisheries Law
Enforcement Command) appear to be too strong. Nevertheless,
some moves towards improved coordination do seem to be
afoot. In November 2012, first reports emerged of the establishment of a 'high-level maritime interests protection office ... with
heads of the related ministries or administrations on board'.[67]
At the same time, a first joint patrol of the South China Sea was
launched, with vessels from the Maritime Safety Administrations

of Guangxi, Guangdong, Fujian and Hainan.[68] When announcing the possibility of more patrols in the South China Sea from Hainanese border police in November 2012, the state-run media also exhorted the police to coordinate more closely with the paramilitaries 'to protect the country's maritime interests'.[69]

Meanwhile, on top of the challenge of coordinating competing actors comes the tyranny of distance. As the Chinese proverb goes, 'the mountains are tall and the emperor is far away'. Beijing continues primarily to measure the performance of local government according to its generation of jobs and GDP growth, and so the intricacies of politics in the provinces bordering the South China Sea, including Guangdong, Shandong, Fujian and Zhejiang, can fly under the radar.

Certainly, the existence of assorted civilian, paramilitary and military actors operating out of various capital, provincial and state-level locations means that there are clear limitations on the extent to which it is sensible to talk of a singular 'China' policy in the South China Sea. Nevertheless, explorations of Beijing's bureaucratic complexities and the consequent dangers of the tail occasionally wagging the dog should only be taken so far. Ultimately, no government is the unitary actor it would wish to be, and issues such as maritime security inevitably cut across multiple departments, regions and responsibilities, not just in China. Such is the reality of policymaking in complex environments. Selective command and control capabilities should not be allowed to obscure ultimate lines of accountability.

Moreover, the array of actors involved is occasionally advantageous for China. The perception of competing agencies can even be a useful tool for Beijing to distance itself from more controversial activities, even as policy is in fact more centrally coordinated. At the very least, actions to police Chinese waters can appear less assertive in their totality when tasks are split between the various functionaries involved. Indeed, one

Chinese commentator described Beijing's orchestration of its assorted actors in the South China Sea as akin to watching a Peking opera.[70] Behind the scenes there is a director, and on stage actors play assorted roles with assorted faces. Drama is carefully and deliberately calculated.

Closely related to the challenge of the bureaucratic coordination of the *number* of policy actors involved is the challenge posed by the *range* of policy interests these actors can represent. This means more than simply competition between agencies for budgets or for specific maritime security responsibilities. It is more about the broad outlook and policy priorities of different institutions, some of which are intimately involved in the South China Sea, and some of which are so only tangentially.

Perhaps traditionally the most transparent clash of cultures and priorities falls between the Ministry of Foreign Affairs (MFA) and the PLA. Where one is focused on serving the national interest through the creation of a peaceful neighbourhood and the cultivation of strong diplomatic ties, the other is focused on serving the national interest through the defence of territorial sovereignty. The MFA has led the way in orchestrating considerable progress in the building of new partnerships in Southeast Asia against a historical background of interference and mistrust. For example, in Cambodia – a country where only a few decades earlier China had been the major foreign patron of the genocidal Khmer Rouge – China is today the most influential foreign power, having been the country's largest investor and biggest aid donor since 1992. In more general terms, Chinese diplomats tend to specialise in a region or even a country, meaning that a Chinese ambassador in the region will often have done at least one previous tour in the country concerned, bringing accompanying linguistic and networking advantages. Furthermore, simple geography means that Chinese leaders can readily participate in a regular programme of high-level visits in support of these ties. In many countries in the region, China is the leading provider of low-interest loans for crucial infrastructure development. For example, in April 2009, Chinese Premier Wen Jiabao announced the creation of a US$10bn China–ASEAN investment cooperation fund to support infrastructure development in the ASEAN region.

Whether or not Beijing's leaders are, as some have suggested, working towards the creation of some sort of Chinese Monroe Doctrine in Southeast Asia, it is clear that sovereignty disputes in the South China Sea serve as a considerable potential drain on the regional good will which Chinese diplomacy has been relatively successful at generating. Of course, there are other issues aside from the South China Sea that cause tension between China and its Southeast Asian neighbours, including hydrography, as, for example, China's moves to dam the Upper Mekong River take downstream effect in the delta. Nevertheless, flows of Chinese trade, bank loans and aid have generally proved better at masking these tensions.

This is not to argue that *all* of China's MFA takes a more moderate approach; clearly there are internal differences of opinion, and a range of views is natural when responsibility for the South China Sea cuts across three separate divisions of the MFA – Asia, Borders and North America (given the US involvement in the region). Nor is it to argue that the MFA is *never* at the forefront of a more assertive stance. Indeed, as previously noted, it was the MFA which deployed the first official use of China's expansive nine-dashed line map in its protest note to the UN following the 2009 joint submission by Malaysia and Vietnam to the Commission on the Limits of the Continental Shelf.[71] But the reality is that Chinese diplomats are generally likely to see the South China Sea disputes within their broader context and to be keener on finding ways to follow Deng's petition to put sovereignty disputes to one side.

In contrast, the PLA's hard-power mandate makes its generally more assertive stance on the disputes almost inevitable. Its growing capabilities might also be inspiring some Chinese adventurism. Some of the toughest statements on Chinese interests and actions in the South China Sea have come from military camps, whether made by serving or, more usually, semi-retired or retired officers. The *People's Liberation Daily* publishes regular examples of this. For example, in 2012, the well-established hawk Major-General Luo Yuan argued in its pages that it was time for China to 'teach the Philippines a lesson', and that, 'if the Philippines cannot rein in their folks, let us discipline them'.[72]

The PLAN in particular is enjoying its time in the sun after a long period of relative neglect. As Beijing's national interests have expanded beyond its borders and cross-strait relations have improved, the focus on Taiwan has slightly diminished. China's increasing dependence on imported oil, combined with its growing range of overseas economic engagements and its status as the world's leading exporter, have understandably stretched old boundaries of understanding as to what constitutes national security. From the ports of Africa and the Middle East to the shipping lanes of the Pacific, Chinese strategy is moving from 'coastal defence' to 'far-sea defence'. A blue-water navy is under creation. After three decades of nearly-continuous double-digit increases in China's defence spending, this very process of modernisation – of strategy as well as equipment – is spreading concern within the region and beyond. At the same time, it is instilling in China's PLA a new sense of self-confidence and pride. The concerns of others are, at times, of limited interest.[73]

Of course, as regional and international attention paid to the South China Sea rises and wanes, so does Chinese central government attention. In other words, effective bureaucratic and policy coordination can lag just behind events, sometimes emerging as a reaction to a situation rather than as a constant in policymaking. One evident danger is therefore the generation of a crisis from below – for example an incident at sea involving paramilitaries that subsequently escalates. Yet, when issues matter to Beijing, the authoritarian state still knows what levers to pull to ensure internal cohesion of action, if not harmony of interest. Meanwhile, the PLA remains very much the power behind the scenes, discharging – even if sometimes at a carefully calculated distance – its mission to 'safeguard the country's sovereign security, territorial integrity and maritime rights'.[74]

## The challenge of managing the PLA

Although it will always be difficult for outsiders to know what precisely is going on inside the black box that is the PLA's decision-making machinery, the division between 'hardline' PLA and 'soft-line' MFA appears too simplistic. The PLA itself is similarly split, in terms of patronage as well as ideas. For example, the PLA has traditionally been the army of the Chinese Communist Party (CCP), rather than the army of the country, as its primary task is to maintain party rule. The defence of national sovereignty follows on from this as another key task. Yet there appears to be increasing recognition within PLA ranks that its military effectiveness would be improved by a calibrated decoupling of this link between party and army. Professional, career soldiers do not all wish to spend up to 30% of their working life in political training. Corruption, which is widely perceived as one of the PLA's biggest challenges and which President Hu labelled in a May 2012 meeting of the Central Military Council as a 'life and death struggle', is also fed by this linkage to the party.[75] Yet the fundamental question of how to make the professionalisation of the PLA compatible with its mandate to serve the CCP first, and how to ensure continued CCP control through any changes, remains unanswered.

In mid-2012, an editorial in the PLA's *People's Liberation Army Daily* even discussed the question of party loyalty, acknowledging what it called 'sub-loyalties' within the military.[76] Although such subjects are always sensitive in years of leadership transition, one impression these discussions give is of a party struggling to establish how much to let its generals speak their minds in an information age, where the outlets interested in their opinions are many but the consumers of news are not always clear on the extent to which such opinions are state-directed. Calls for China to do more to defend its interests on the international stage, including through the selective use of hard-power capabilities, encourage confusion among foreign observers and local readers alike over the level of official sponsorship behind these more provocative and populist statements. In the process, suspicious outsiders can find justification for their concerns about the challenges of China's rise and their prescription of a hardline response, at the same time as local nationalists can find themselves encouraged further to voice provocative, and indeed aggressive, opinions. As these action–reaction dynamics develop, so mistrust deepens.

Indeed, the profusion of military media commentators that the PLA has been developing since the late 1990s for what it has described as public opinion warfare operations (*yunlan zhan*) has certainly complicated the interpretation of Beijing's actual positioning (as opposed to its diplomatic positioning).[77] The basic aim of 'public opinion warfare' is to generate domestic popular support for China's position and opposition to China's enemies. So when a PLA official, whether semi-retired like Yang Yi, or still serving, like Dai Xu, urges the Chinese government to take a tougher line in defending its interests in the South China Sea, are they conducting 'public opinion warfare operations' on behalf of the PLA as approved by the government, providing evidence of a growing civil–military divide, or acting as conduits for conservative factions within the PLA? Or are they speaking simply for themselves or furthering their pundit careers, albeit with some level of prior clearance?[78] The answer appears, frustratingly, to be a mixture of all of the above.

There are also obvious difficulties in managing public messaging for different domestic and international audiences. For example, when the *People's Liberation Daily* publishes a commentary warning against US 'meddling and intervention' in the South China Sea should the US wish to avoid 'resolution through armed force', was it accurate for Reuters to report this story as China's 'toughest high-level warning yet'?[79] Or was, perhaps, the inference of senior, official backing for such a 'high-level warning' a little unfair? Certainly, there are those even within the PLA who are dismissive of some of their more hawkish colleagues on the South China Sea, but the rules of 'public opinion warfare operations' appear to mean that such voices rarely attract serious public exposure. Perhaps this is somewhat reflective of an understandable lack of enthusiasm on the part of moderates to expose themselves to the vitriol of popular nationalists, but it is likely also reflective of where the bias in government sponsorship and thinking falls. In other words, the mainstream might not be quite as moderate as outsiders are often reassured is actually the case.

Certainly, PLA influence on Chinese foreign and security policymaking remains substantive. The PLA may have only two seats on the 18th Politburo and none on its Standing Committee, but with just over 20% of the CCP's Central Committee, it is a powerful influence within a factionalised party, particularly at a time of leadership transition.[80] How coherent this influence is remains unclear, but the trend does appear to be towards the more assertive, even allowing for the likelihood that the more hawkish views of retired military officers in particular can be used as test balloons for policymaking, and even, on occasion, as deliberate outlets for the channelling of popular frustration. For example, in July 2012, the new political commissar of the PLAN's South Sea Fleet was announced as being the 'famously hawkish' Vice-Admiral Wang Dengping.[81] Months earlier, Wang had warned that, 'we, as navy officers, should not let our territory be diminished on our watch, and we should not let our lands be lost'.[82] Soon after, a major reshuffle of military units in Hainan province was announced, including a new political commissar and a new head of the political department. Speaking at the announcement, Lieutenant-General Xu Fenlin, the commander of the Guangzhou Military Command which oversees Hainan, called attention to the province's 'unprecedented responsibility and pressure' in defending China's sovereignty in the South China Sea, asking the provincial military region to make 'solid preparations for military conflicts to fulfil the missions bestowed upon it by the party and the people'.[83] Meanwhile, it remains conceivable, if unproven, that some of the CCP's civilian leadership is increasingly comfortable utilising the leverage provided by the improved military capabilities that their funding decisions have developed – and which now look increasingly fit for purpose – as a potential tool of foreign policy.[84]

## Managing or directing popular nationalism?

Assertive posturing is not confined simply to the op-ed pages of the military papers. CCP newspapers such as *China Daily* and *People's Daily* are also prone to the simultaneous reflection and cultivation of nationalist opinion. For example, in mid-2012, a by-lined article in *China Daily* argued that China had, for a long time, shown restraint in the disputes, but that this restraint was being taken advantage of by rival claimants. It concluded that, 'if China's constant diplomatic claims won't work anymore, it must consider effective alternatives'.[85] Meanwhile, a senior editor of the *People's Daily* echoed the views of an amorphous but influential conservative faction advocating the drawing of red lines in the South China Sea when he argued, 'we have to draw a set of lines [in the South China Sea] for the United States to alert the Americans regarding what it can do and what it cannot'.[86] Less than two weeks after China agreed guidelines with ASEAN for the management of sovereignty disputes in the South China Sea in July 2011, a front-page commentary in the *People's Daily* ended with a warning to the Philippines for 'violating China's territorial sovereignty': 'those who make serious strategic misjudgements on this issue will pay the appropriate price'.[87] Indeed, in 2010, *People's Daily* published 325 articles on the South China Sea compared to an average of one article per year in the two decades between 1980 and 2000.[88]

The existence of popular nationalism supporting Chinese claims in the South China Sea is undeniable. Microblogs, in particular, provide repeated reminders of the vehemence with which discussions can be conducted, serving to underline why it is that even the management of these competing claims can prove so tricky, with any ambitions of resolution remaining a long way off. When, in May 2012, a presenter for state-run Chinese Central Television (CCTV) mistakenly referred to the whole of the Philippines as being a part of China, as opposed to simply referencing Scarborough Reef, the clip of her comments may have quickly been removed from CCTV's website but it proliferated elsewhere as bloggers revelled in her comment. 'We all know that the Philippines is China's inherent territory and the Philippines belongs to Chinese sovereignty, this is an indisputable fact', one blogger argued, whilst another offered his own suggestion for dispute resolution: 'If every Chinese spat once, we could drown [the Philippines]'.[89]

As party propaganda repeatedly reminds its citizens of China's growing capabilities, it is no surprise that some wish to see these capabilities more assertively deployed in defence of perceived national interests. Those inclined to take a more conciliatory line find themselves denounced as 'traitors' or 'eunuchs'. For example, in 2004, nationalist netizens in China established a website 'Nansha Online' aimed at increasing public awareness for China's 'lost territories' in the South China Sea. Amongst other entries, a list of 'traitors' has been compiled detailing academics, officials and commentators perceived to be too weak in their protection of Chinese interests in the sea.[90]

The danger here is that nationalist opinion in any particular country threatens to undermine a government's ability to control its foreign policy actively. In Vietnam and China, in particular, where nationalism is encouraged through historical education, occasional paroxysms of nationalistic protests are initially tacitly encouraged, before being subsequently oppressed. Although the initial outpouring of nationalist credentials can be therapeutic for the populace and even supportive of the government's foreign-policy aims, the subsequent shut-down results from the danger that such nationalist displays can also limit policy options. Nationalism also carries the risk that it may potentially transmogrify into unrest directed against the government itself, should it be perceived as being too weak or should the protests harness other underlying discontent among the unrepresented populations. Popular nationalism can also incite reactions among rivals, hence further escalating a particular dispute, and can therefore be counterproductive to a country's particular aims.[91] In such circumstances, national media can be deployed to deescalate situations. As

Beijing indulged in some diplomatic damage control following a period of more assertive behaviour, in late 2011-early 2012, the *People's Daily* ran a series of columns noting the advantages of 'pragmatic cooperation' in the South China Sea in order to achieve 'concrete results'.[92]

However, the domestic popular reaction within China to rival claimant posturing as well as US surveillance activities in the South China Sea is different in nature from the nationalism surrounding 'core' issues such as Tibet and Taiwan. It is also potentially more manageable in substance than the nationalism directed against other foreigners with regard to the management of sovereignty claims in the East China Sea, where nationalist sentiment against Japanese claims continues to run high.[93] Certainly the pride of being a rising or returning power – whose people are repeatedly told about their centre-stage role in the twenty-first century – and the memory by that same power of a previous 'century of humiliation', provides an important undercurrent for nationalism in the South China Sea, and elsewhere. But the handling of this nationalism on the part of the CCP does little to convince onlookers that China's leadership has the political will to challenge such thinking and more to feed suspicions that it might simply find it more convenient, at least in the short term, even to cultivate it. Moves such as the decision by the 2012 session of the National People's Congress to mandate the instruction of school pupils on Chinese territory in the South China Sea, or the June 2010 planting of a Chinese flag on the bed of the South China Sea, do little to inspire confidence.[94] The proliferation of nationalist comments across the Chinese blogosphere on the stand-off with the Philippines at Scarborough Reef was nonetheless revealing when contrasted to the simultaneous heavy censorship exerted over comments of China's handling of civil-rights activist Chen Guangcheng and his move to the US.[95]

## Beijing's South China Sea campaign

There are, then, a number of factors constraining China's room for manoeuvre in the prosecution of its sovereignty claims in the South China Sea, as well as a number of factors mitigating the effectiveness of the tactics it does chose to pursue. Nevertheless, whilst awareness of the range of actors involved and the different interests that are contributing to policymaking is important, it is also necessary to guard against an over-emphasis on the complexities of Beijing's policymaking scene. As this chapter has argued, questions of maritime security are, by definition, cross cutting, involving the coordination of civil and military, as well as national and regional, components. In this regard, Beijing's challenges are not substantively different from those faced by others. Moreover, it seems clear that Beijing is absolutely aware of the impressive range of levers it has at its disposal, and is seeking carefully to balance its assorted interests in the South China Sea by calculated and calibrated deployment of them. Claims of sovereignty are consequently energetically pushed by an array of actors resulting in continued but careful encroachments that run against the spirit if not the letter of the DoC. Meanwhile, China's responses to US surveillance activities now encompass more direct military and paramilitary action alongside continued diplomatic protests.

Likewise, although it is important to understand perspectives from Beijing – where China is often perceived to be the reactionary victim of more assertive actions by others – the sheer strength and reach of China's capabilities relative to the other claimants incur on it certain responsibilities in the management of these action–reaction dynamics. Moreover Beijing has repeatedly demonstrated an ability to use this dynamic to its advantage, operating an array of probing tactics that have variously been referred to by foreign commentators as 'salami slicing', 'good cop, bad cop' and 'talk and take'.

As China looks to advance its national interests, the South China Sea is inevitably attracting attention both in terms of its significance for the country's national security and its prospects for future economic development. How China manages, and is perceived to manage, these interests, and the tensions they are generating both within the region and beyond, will say a lot about the role China intends to play, and is able to play, in the region more generally. In the face of perception and misperception, action and reaction, the message for Beijing is an empowering but daunting one: ultimately, China remains the master of its own fate in the South China Sea.

In the end, China's continued interest in the peace and security of the region means that it aims to push rather than break limits. Although time appears to be on its side, China is not a status quo power in the region. But nor, despite the range of strategies outlined in this chapter, is China the only power involved in setting the tempo and substance for dispute management in the South China Sea. As the next chapter goes on to explore, other regional actors in Southeast Asia are not simply bystanders to China's rise and the consequent drama of great-power relations surrounding the South China Sea.

## Notes

1  Trefor Moss, 'China's Not-So-Hard Power Strategy', *The Diplomat*, 28 June 2012, http://thediplomat.com/2012/06/28/chinas-not-so-hard-power-strategy/.

2  For example, Moss credits China for not escalating conflict by introducing PLAN vessels, but instead relying on paramilitaries to project Chinese presence. However, it is worth noting that in the instance he cites at Scarborough Reef, it was Chinese fishing vessels acting illegally – which the Philippine authorities then attempted to arrest, albeit in a somewhat heavy handed manner – that triggered the whole stand-off.

3  A parallel argument was made when Chen Shui-bian was in power in Taiwan. China only behaved as it did, because Chen was forcing it to.

4  See, for example: Michael D. Swaine and M. Taylor Fravel, 'China's Assertive Behaviour – Part Two: The Maritime Periphery', *China*

*Leadership Monitor*, no. 35, Summer 2011, http://media.hoover.org/sites/default/files/documents/CLM35MS.pdf.

5   The incoming Chinese ambassador to ASEAN, Yang Xiuping, used the phrase 'core interests' while speaking at the Asia-Pacific Roundtable in Kuala Lumpur in May 2012. 'China-Philippines Cooperation Depends on Proper Settlement of Maritime Disputes', Xinhua News Agency, 31 August 2011.

6   See: Swaine and Fravel, 'China's Assertive Behaviour – Part One: China's 'Core Interests', *China Leadership Monitor*, no. 34, Winter 2011, http://media.hoover.org/sites/default/files/documents/CLM34MS.pdf.

7   Minnie Chan, 'Beijing Lists Unity and Security as Core Interests', *South China Morning Post*, 7 September 2011, http://www.scmp.com/article/978288/beijing-lists-unity-and-security-core-interests.

8   Storey, 'China's Bilateral and Multilateral Diplomacy in the South China Sea', p. 56.

9   Cronin and Kaplan, 'Cooperation from Strength: U.S. Strategy and the South China Sea', p. 25.

10  Zhong Sheng, 'Hold Mainstream of China–ASEAN Relations', *People's Daily Online*, 6 April 2012, http://english.peopledaily.com.cn/90780/7779588.html.

11  Quoted in: 'Full Unclosure?', *The Economist*, 24 March 2012, http://www.economist.com/node/21551113.

12  Liang Guanglie, 'A Better Future Through Security Cooperation', speech at the Shangri-La Dialogue, Singapore, 5 June 2011.

Available at: http://www.iiss.org/conferences/the-shangri-la-dialogue/shangri-la-dialogue-2011/speeches/fourth-plenary-session/general-liang-guanglie-english/.

13  Pia Lee Brago, 'New Chinese Envoy sees Peaceful Solution to Spratlys Dispute', *The Philippine Star*, 22 February 2012, http://www.philstar.com/headlines/779568/new-chinese-envoy-sees-peaceful-solution-spratlys-dispute.

14  IISS Shangri-La Dialogue discussions, 2 June 2012.

15  Xue Hanqin, lecture at the Institute of South East Asian Studies, Singapore, 19 November 2009.

16  See, for example: Zhong Sheng, 'Hold Mainstream of China–ASEAN Relations', *People's Daily*, 9 April 2012. Similar comments were made by Wen Jiabao during the 20th ASEAN Summit in Bali in November 2011, warning that disputes should be discussed only amongst claimants and rejecting the involvement of 'outside powers'.

17  Interview with Chinese think tanker, IISS Shangri-La Dialogue, 2 June 2012. Lack of Chinese interest in negotiating a follow-up Code with ASEAN through 2012 appears to confirm this interpretation.

18  Six-Point Agreement between China and Vietnam to guide settlement of maritime disputes, 11 October 2011. As reported, for example, by *Xinhua* on 12 October 2012.

19  'China Envoy to Philippines Airs Views on Spratlys', *Manila Bulletin*, 23 December 2010.

20  Jerry Esplanada, 'Okay to Buy Warships but don't bring US into Spratly Dispute', *Philippine Daily Inquirer*, 23 February 2012.

21  *Romeo-* and *Whiskey*-class sub-marines formed the backbone of China's fleet in the late 1980s, while *Luda*-class destroyers and *Jianghu*-class frigates were both based on 1950s Soviet designs. For a listing of China's late Cold War fleet, see: *The Military Balance 1988–89*, (London: IISS, 1989), pp. 149–50.

22  Fravel, 'Maritime Security in the South China Sea and the Competition over Maritime Rights', in Cronin (ed.), *Cooperation from Strength*, p. 40.

23  A point appreciated by Deputy Chief of the PLA General Zhang Li in his 2009 call for China to establish an air and sea port on Mischief Reef. For more on this argument, see: Leszek Buszynski, 'The South China Sea: Oil, Maritime Claims, and U.S.–China Strategic Rivalry', *Washington Quarterly*, vol. 35, no. 2, Spring 2012, p. 146.

24  Fravel, 'Maritime Security in the South China Sea and the Competition over Maritime Rights', p. 41.

25  Chan, 'PLA Navy in Live-fire Attack Drills in East China and South China Seas', SCMP, 18 January 2013.

26  For a description of A2AD and the US pivot to Asia, see; 'New US Military Concept Marks Pivot to Sea and Air', IISS *Strategic Comments*, vol. 18, no. 20, May 2012; and Christian Le Mière, 'America's Pivot to East Asia: The Naval Dimension', *Survival*, vol. 54, no. 3, June–July 2012, pp. 81–94.

27  Toshi Yoshihara and James Holmes, 'Small Stick Diplomacy in the South China Sea', *The National Interest*, 23 April 2012.

28  For a fuller description of China's five maritime paramilitary agencies, see: Christian Le Mière, 'Policing the Waves: Maritime Paramilitaries in the Asia-Pacific', *Survival*, vol. 53, no. 1, December 2010–January 2011, pp. 133–46.

29  It is also important that the little stick of diplomacy of the paramili-taries is supported by a bigger stick of the PLAN in the background. For example, it was only CMS vessels that entered the waters around the disputed Senkaku/Diaoyu Islands in the East China Sea in September 2012, which may have indicated a desire to limit escalation on China's behalf, yet the fact that an anti-ship missiles test occurred in the East China Sea in the same month was a deliberate and complementary reminder of China's military capabilities.

30  'China Patrols S China Sea to Fight Illegal Exploration', *People's Daily Online*, 20 March 2012, http://english.peopledaily.com.cn/90883/7762726.html.

31  'China Beefs Up its Offshore Law Enforcement', *China Daily*, 18 September 2010, http://www.chinadaily.com.cn/china/2010-09/18/content_11320201.htm.

32  In this incident, the Philippines also behaved more assertively in the deployment of a warship to make the arrests. Although the Philippines argued that this was more a matter of geography than a deliberate escalation (the warship was apparently their closest vessel to the incident) it was clear from reactions amongst the Philippines' fellow ASEAN member states that they at least were not convinced. Two days later Manila did however replace the warship with a coast-guard vessel.

33 Chinese sources repeatedly note that Beijing regularly requests the US to desist from such surveillance activities off its shores but to no effect. The subsequent move to a more aggressive form of protest is therefore seen, at least from Beijing's perspective, as a reasonable counter-action to ongoing US hostility.

34 According to Shirley Kan, 'the PLA had started aggressive interceptions of U.S. reconnaissance flights in December 2000'. *US–China Military Contacts: Issues for Congress*, Congressional Research Service, 19 June 2012.

35 'China-ASEAN Free Trade Area Starts Operation', Xinhua, 1 January 2010. Bilateral trade volume between China and ASEAN reached US$362.9bn in 2011, a rise of 24% of 2010. 'China–ASEAN Embrace Growing Trade Volume', *CNS*, 17 January 2012.

36 By 2012, bilateral trade between China and the Philippines was already not far approaching bilateral trade between the US and the Philippines, whilst in 2011 a target of doubling bilateral trade to US$60bn a year by 2016 was agreed between China and the Philippines. Cheng Guangjin and Lan Lan, 'Sino-Philippine Trade to Double', *China Daily*, 1 September 2011.

37 The initial health warning was sent several weeks before the beginning of the stand-off at Scarborough but it was targeted only at fruit from a single conglomerate operating in Mindanao with no curbs on imports attached. Two months later, China's General Administration of Quality Supervision, Inspection and Quarantine noted that it had found 104 types of 'harmful organisms' in fruit arriving from the Philippines. Andrew Higgins, 'In Philippines, Banana Growers Feel Effects of South China Sea Disputes', *Washington Post*, 10 June 2012, http://articles.washingtonpost.com/2012-06-10/world/35461588_1_chinese-fishermen-president-benigno-aquino-iii-south-china-sea.

38 *Ibid.*

39 Exports to China by trading partners whose leaders met with the Dalai Lama fell on average between 8.1% and 16.9% following such a meeting. For more on this argument, see, for example: Andreas Fuchs and Nils-Hendrik Klann, 'Paying a Visit: The Dalai Lama Effect on International Trade', Research Paper no. 113, Center for European Governance and Economic Development, 19 October 2010.

40 Will Rogers, 'The Role of Natural Resources in the South China Sea', in Cronin (ed.), *Cooperation from Strength*, p. 86. Figures taken from: the BP 'Statistical Review of World Energy', June 2011, p. 6.

41 Leslie Hook, 'Gas Finds Give Impetus to China Sea claim', *Financial Times*, 9 November 2012, http://www.ft.com/cms/s/0/a782a6f8-2a73-11e2-a137-00144feabdc0.html#axzz2JTyEEgny.

42 There is also an important distinction over what proportion of these reserves is recoverable in terms of economic viability or technological capabilities. Chinese estimates of oil reserves in the South China Sea can be upwards of 100bn barrels. In contrast, an estimate released by the US Energy Information Administration in 2013 suggests reserves of around 11bn barrels.

43 Fravel, 'Maritime Security in the South China Sea and the Competition over Maritime Rights', p. 36.

44 The same is true of Chinese operations against Vietnamese and Philippine fishing vessels. Periods of tight enforcement, arrests and ransoms, are followed by periods of relative calm.

45 Fravel, 'The South China Sea Oil Card', *The Diplomat*, 27 June 2012, http://thediplomat.com/china-power/the-south-china-sea-oil-card/. It should also be noted that the disputed status of these blocks means that it is likely that interest from foreign oil companies is limited. The move could therefore be more symbolic than substantive.

46 Mark Valencia, 'China Upsets Asia's Applecart', *Japan Times*, 11 July 2012.

47 In May 2012, China's first deep-water oil drill began operations in undisputed waters 320km southeast of Hong Kong. As the technology is tried and tested it is reasonable to expect exploitation in contested waters will at least be mooted.

48 Brian Spegele and Wayne Ma, 'For China Boss, Deep-water Rigs are a "Strategic Weapon"', *Wall Street Journal*, 29 August 2012, http://online.wsj.com/article/SB10000872396390442331045775928907387402 90.html.

49 Michael Richardson, 'China's Gunboat Diplomacy', *Japan Times*, 30 July 2012. The original comment was made in an article by He Jianbin in *Global Times* on 28 June 2012.

50 Huang Yiming and Jin Haixing, 'Fishing Vessels set off for Nansha Islands', *China Daily*, 13 July 2012, http://www.chinadaily.com.cn/china/2012-07/13/content_15575461.htm.

51 For more on this, see: Zhang Hongzhou, 'China's Evolving Fishing Industry: Implications for Regional and Global Maritime Security', RSIS Working Paper 246, 16 August 2012, in particular see p. 8. See also: 'State of World Fisheries and Aquaculture 2010', UN Food and Agriculture Organisation, Rome, 2010, http://www.fao.org/docrep/013/i1820e/i1820e.pdf.

52 In March 2009, China formally announced that one reason for the conduct of patrols by Fisheries Administration vessels was to demonstrate sovereignty.

53 According to Xinhua, Sansha 'administers over 200 islets' and '2 million square kilometres of water'. James Webb, 'The South China Sea's Gathering Storm', *Wall Street Journal*, 20 August 2012, http://online.wsj.com/article/SB10000872396390444184704577587483914661256.html.

54 For an example of this link between Vietnamese and Chinese actions, see: Teddy Ng, 'New City to Run Disputed Island Chains', *South China Morning Post*, 22 June 2012.

55 June Teufel Dreyer, 'Sansha: New City in the South China Sea', *China Brief*, vol. 12, no. 16, 17 August 2012.

56 See Christian Le Mière and Sarah Raine, 'Water Pollution: South China Sea Dispute Taints the Region', *Jane's Intelligence Review*, February 2013.

57 'China to Officially Name Islands in Sovereignty Move', Xinhua, 16 October 2012.

58 Both countries issued visas instead on separate pieces of paper.

59 'New Chinese Passports "Counter-productive"', Channel News Asia, 29 November 2012.

60 Again, Beijing is not the only claimant encouraging new inhabitants and visitors to the islands. The southern Vietnamese province of Khanh Hoa – which has administrative responsibility for the islands within Vietnam – has organised a delegation of Buddhist monks for a six-month curatorship of recently refurbished temples on Vietnamese-held islands in the Spratly grouping. 'Vietnam to send Buddhist Monks to Spratly Islands', *BBC News*, 12 March 2012, http://www.bbc.co.uk/news/world-asia-17343596.

61 'China to Develop Tourism on Xisha Islands', *China Daily*, 12 March 2012. There is some confusion on the precise nature of any plans. For example, on 6 April 2012, *Beijing Times* and *Shanghai Daily* both quoted China's tourism authority now denying previous reports of sightseeing tours launching soon. On the same day, *Beijing News* reported that Hainan was still pressing ahead with its tourism-promotion plans.

62 'Chinese Cruise Ship Returns from Trial Xisha Voyage', *People's Daily Online*, 10 April 2012, http://english. peopledaily.com.cn/90882/7782605. html.

63 Prepared Statement by Fravel to a US House Committee on Foreign Affairs on 'Investigating the China Threat, Part One: Military and Economic Aggression', 28 March 2012.

64 International Crisis Group, 'Stirring up the South China Sea (1)', Asia Report no. 223, 23 April 2012.

65 For more details on these five agencies, see: 'Five Dragons Stirring up the Sea', *Maritime Study no.5*, US Naval War College, April 2010; and Christian Le Mière, 'Policing the Waves'.

66 These suggestions, made by Luo Yuan in March 2012, may not reflect official policy but may be further evidence of retired Chinese generals acting to test publicly the waters for new policies. Interview with Luo in 'Coast Guard Missing Piece of Naval Strength', *Global Times*, 8 March 2012, http://www. globaltimes.cn/NEWS/tabid/99/ ID/699279/Coast-guard-missing-piece-of-naval-strength.aspx.

67 Wang Qian, 'Cross-province Patrol Begins in South China Sea', *China Daily*, 9 November 2012, http://www.chinadaily.com.cn/ cndy/2012-11/09/content_15899201. htm.

68 *Ibid.*

69 Qian, 'Hainan Border Police Given New Powers', *China Daily*, 28 November 2012.

70 Interview with Chinese academic, Singapore, 4 June 2012.

71 Note from the PRC's permanent mission to the UN, 7 May 2009, http://www.un.org/Depts/los/ clcs_new/submissions_files/ mysvnm33_09/chn_2009re_mys_ vnm_e.pdf.

72 *Global Times*, 23 May 2012, quoted in: Willy Lam, 'China Deploys Pugilistic Foreign Policy with New Vigour', *China Brief*, vol. 12, no. 12, 22 June 2012.

73 If China's military modernisation causes insecurities in others, there is only so much China can and should do. Interview at the National

Defence University, Beijing, September 2010.

74 Defence Ministry spokesman, quoted in: 'Chinese Defence Ministry Vows to Safeguard Maritime Rights', Xinhua, 28 June 2012.

75 General Liu Yuan is one example of a PLA officer who has been relatively outspoken in this regard. Stories of PLA corruption abound. See, for example, the removal of Lt.-Gen. Gu Junshan for the embezzlement of hundreds of millions of US dollars.

76 See, for example, the report by *Trusted Sources* that quotes from this article in *People's Liberation Army Daily* on 17 June 2012. 'Keeping the Army in Step', *Trusted Sources*, 22 June 2012, http://www.trustedsources.co.uk/blog/china/keeping-the-army-in-step.

77 See, for example: 'Chinese People's Liberation Army Political Work Regulations' [zhongguo renmin jiefangjun zhengzhi gongzuo tiaoli] from 2003.

78 For an example of Yang Yi's hawkish rhetoric, see: Xinhua's interview of 26 December 2011: 'When any country infringes upon our nation's security and interests, we must stage a resolute self-defence.' Counter-attack measures should 'leave no room for ambiguity'.

79 Chris Buckley, 'China Military Warns of Confrontation over Seas', Reuters, 21 April 2012.

80 Peter Mattis, 'How Much Power Does China's 'People's Army' Have?', *The Diplomat*, 13 July 2012, http://thediplomat.com/china-power/how-much-power-does-chinas-peoples-army-have/. In the 18th Politburo, the PLA is represented (aside from by General Secretary and CMC Chair Xi Jinping) by CMC Vice Chairs Fan Chanlong and Xu Qiliang.

81 Ng, 'Hawkish Commander Heads South Sea Fleet', *South China Morning Post*, 10 July 2012.

82 *Ibid.*

83 Ng, 'Reshuffle Linked to Island Disputes', *South China Morning Post*, 12 July 2012.

84 For more on this argument, see: J. Michael Cole, 'Militarization of China's Civilian Leaders?', *The Diplomat*, 29 August 2012. http://thediplomat.com/china-power/the-militarization-of-chinas-civilian-leaders/.

85 Ming Yang, 'Taking Advantage of China's Peaceful Stance', *China Daily*, 30 June 2012, http://www.chinadaily.com.cn/opinion/2012-06/30/content_15539033.htm.

86 Ding Gang, *People's Daily*, 2 June 2012, as cited by: Lam, 'China Deploys Pugilistic Foreign Policy with New Vigor', *China Brief*, vol. 12, no. 12, 22 June 2012.

87 Cited by: Yoichi Kato, 'South China Sea Disputes: Harbinger of Regional Strategic Shift?', *AJISS-Commentary*, no. 130, 14 September 2011.

88 Francesco Guarascio, 'Europe Ignoring Geopolitical Flashpoint of South China Sea', *Public Service Europe*, 2 April 2012.

89 'Philippines belongs to China: CCTV', *Taipei Times*, 10 May 2012, http://www.taipeitimes.com/News/front/archives/2012/05/10/2003532435.

90 The website is www.nansha.org. The list of 'traitors' can be found at: http://www.nansha.org/forum/viewtopic.php?f=3&t=3778&sid=39e499c0b48c434b9126a0c439253e49

91  For a discussion of nationalism in East Asia, see: Christian Le Mière, 'Games Countries Play', *Survival*, vol. 54, no. 5, October–November 2012, pp. 250–56.

92  Fravel, 'All Quiet in the South China Sea', *Foreign Affairs*, 22 March 2012. The example cited is from a column by Zhong Sheng, published in *The People's Daily* in January 2012.

93  Nationalist displays with regard to these core issues are different in part because the targets, whether Tibetans and Taiwanese, are fundamentally perceived to be Chinese. In sovereignty disputes in both the East China and South China Sea, the targets of such displays are 'foreigners'. This in turn introduces a further action–reaction dynamic.

94  Guarascio, 'Europe Ignoring Geopolitical Flashpoint of South China Sea'; 'China Plants Flag in South Sea Amid Disputes', Reuters, 26 August 2010.

95  It is of course possible that the two are linked, and that the approval of nationalist sentiment in the South China Sea can be useful as a valve to diffuse and distract from problems elsewhere. See, for example: Damian Grammaticas, 'China Bangs the War Drum over the South China Sea', *BBC News*, 10 May 2012, http://www.bbc.co.uk/news/world-asia-china-18016901.

# CHAPTER THREE

# Southeast Asia – between emerging great-power rivalry

The smaller and medium-sized powers of Southeast Asia are experienced hosts of great-power influence and competition. The legacy of centuries of cultural and economic influence from China, India and the Middle East, as well as European colonisation, continues to be much in evidence within the region today. During the Cold War, as conflict raged in Indochina and insurgencies plagued most of today's ASEAN states, competition between militaries and ideologies was similarly on full display. Yet in the wake of the departure of US combat forces from Vietnam in 1973, Southeast Asia was left to develop relatively unencumbered by such attentions. For the past 20 years, albeit to differing degrees, its countries have generally found ways to work with the US as the established regional hegemon, whilst aiming to ensure some degree of regional autonomy of action. Indeed, arguably part of the driving force behind Southeast Asia's devotion to the concept of ASEAN centrality emanates from a desire to protect this autonomy, with the intention that regional concerns – as opposed to the concerns of outside powers – may continue to occupy centre-stage. And in this regard at least, ASEAN has enjoyed some success –

although it could also be argued that this focus has come at the price of limiting its regional efficacy.

Meanwhile, the mechanisms for the extension of great-power influence within Southeast Asia have also evolved with the centuries. Hard power still has its place, including through the web of military alliances and partnerships that have grown up across the region. But new channels for influence have also arisen, in particular through the 'explosion of diplomatic forums' that are in evidence throughout the region, as well as in the opportunities afforded by the liberalisation of the global economic order.[1] As China has re-emerged as an increasingly important regional influence, in particular through its economic and diplomatic interactions in the region, so a debate has developed on the role of 'balance of power' politics in today's Southeast Asia. For some, such as Amitav Acharya, the concept is of less use today than in past times: 'Asia is increasingly able to manage its insecurity through shared regional norms, rising economic interdependence, and growing institutional linkages'.[2] Meanwhile, for structural realists such as Robert Ross, the realities of power balancing are stronger than ever, with the region unable to escape from the fundamental security dilemma of concern over China's underlying intentions. Perhaps inevitably then, Ross sees a pattern whereby mainland states are increasingly bowing to China's might, whilst maritime states remain more committed to a balancing act that includes helping America preserve its maritime ascendancy.[3]

More generally, China's rise sparked a lively debate on whether the countries of Southeast Asia would balance against or bandwagon with China, and how their respective decisions on this front would impact on their relations with other major powers in the region. This debate soon matured into a recognition that the game in Southeast Asia is precisely about not having to choose between the US and China. The aim is neither to balance nor bandwagon. At its most ambitious, it is about how actively to help shape an inclusive regional order which keeps key powers engaged and to maximum regional benefit. Outlining his support for a Code of Conduct on the South China Sea in November 2011, Indonesian Foreign Minister Marty Natalegawa noted that: 'ASEAN will not let the region become a competition arena for countries who consider themselves as big powers, whoever and whenever they may be.'[4] Instead, the aim is to enmesh competing great powers sufficiently in the region's economic and diplomatic affairs so as to give them a clear stake in regional cooperation, growth and stability.

Although there have, of course, been a range of responses and strategies on display by the nation-states of Southeast Asia, the general policy response has been one that is often conceived of as a dual-track approach. This involves the generation of an inclusive regional order where all are welcome to participate in the web of economic ties engendered by increasingly liberal economic policies and underpinned by established international norms. At the same time, regional powers can be seen hedging against disorder through the development of their own military capabilities and the shoring up of their great-power alliances. This usually involves some degree of ongoing hard-power engagement with the US and China. The relative degrees of such engagement with both vary, and not always predictably so, and engagement with China is noticeably more limited, at least for the moment.[5]

This cooperation is deliberately constrained. A significant permanent footprint from any extra-regional power has traditionally been resisted in line with the 1971 declaration of a Zone of Peace, Freedom and Neutrality, which asks for the region both to 'broaden cooperation' but also be 'kept free from any form or manner of interference by outside powers'.[6]

Former Singaporean Prime Minister Lee Kuan Yew encapsulated this approach when he suggested that Southeast Asian states should pragmatically 'engage, not contain, China, but ... also quietly ... set pieces into place for a fall-back position should China not play in accordance with the rules as a good global citizen'.[7]

Despite their smaller size, Southeast Asian nations have some collective leverage as a result of their strategic significance (including, from a post-9/11 US perspective, in terms of the battle against terrorism), as well as from a resource and trading perspective (lying as they do at the crossroads of some of the world's most important sea lanes). With some of the world's fastest-growing economies and a combined population of more than 580 million people, they are also of increasing collective economic significance. For example, the China–ASEAN Free Trade Area which came into being in January 2010 comprises the world's largest free-trade area by population and the third largest by GDP. Indeed, in private, many Southeast Asian officials readily concede that stable competition between regional powers – not just the US and China but also including Japan and India – can offer opportunities for leverage which are very much in the interests of these smaller and medium-sized powers. Southeast Asian nations are not then, as is sometimes portrayed, simply the passive victims of great-power politics. Instead they are increasingly engaged in more strategic considerations over how best to protect their respective national interests, which lie in the avoidance of both conflict and an exclusionary condominium.

Southeast Asian nations have been particularly taken up by this challenge since the end of the Cold War, when the region was seen by some as ripe for instability: the US would withdraw its attentions, China would rise, Japan remilitarise and Southeast Asian nations fall into an arms race.[8] Although a continuing US presence in the region has added greatly to its stability, Southeast Asian nations should also be credited with some modest strategic successes in this regard. Acting on their own profound ambivalence about the rise of China, many have worked to enmesh the great powers within the region – including institutionally, for example, through the East Asia Summit – as well as to be quietly supportive of continued US engagement.[9] They have also been active in engaging China, driven primarily and pragmatically by the lure of closer economic ties, but with a secondary eye on socialisation – conscious of their own role in the cultivation of China as a responsible regional power with sufficient space to grow that it feels able to develop within existing norms rather than to seek the creation of a new order.

However, the focus has not only been engaging the US and China. In recent years, attentions have expanded to include the development of exchanges and cooperation with other powers, such as India, Japan and South Korea. Given its questionable impact as an effective check on Chinese behaviour, the development of an ASEAN Regional Forum may have proved a frustrating talking-shop to some, but even this talking, within an institutionalised structure, can serve a diplomatic purpose for ASEAN member states. Meanwhile, its prioritisation of consensus also helps level the playing field among member states with starkly different reaches and capabilities, potentially allowing smaller but strategically minded countries, such as Singapore, a greater opportunity for influence.[10] Furthermore, the complex web of balancing interactions this multi-directional approach helps create is strategically advantageous to Southeast Asian nations who are not just concerned with US–China relations, but also with relations between themselves. Laos, to take one example, seeks not simply to avoid undue influence from China, but also from Thailand and

Vietnam. Meanwhile, Singapore's military development has been as much, if not more, influenced by traditional tensions with Malaysia and Indonesia as by the rise of China. Lastly and importantly, this inclusive approach also helps build in economic resilience at a crucial stage in the development of these countries.

Tensions would then exist around the South China Sea, even without the existence of assorted sovereignty disputes within these waters. Regional suspicions about the ultimate intent and effect of China's military modernisation would endure. The US would anyway be looking to shore up its engagement in a region of the world that is increasingly important both economically and geopolitically. Yet this sea is fast becoming a particular regional pivot, as the disputes provide a focal point for attention. China's heavy-handed pursuit of its sovereignty claims in the sea around 2009–10 resulted, for example, in certain Southeast Asian countries being more solicitous of US engagement in the region.[11] Meanwhile Beijing's decision to escalate its protests at the activities of US military vessels off Chinese shores to the level of confrontation also helped focus US minds on the sea, including on the broader implications for US naval power of the dispute over freedom of passage within EEZs. Lastly, globalisation and the rise of Asia in general have helped highlight the particular strategic significance of the shipping lanes that run through this sea, further increasing the stakes for ensuring access to them, and ultimately control over them.

## Regional approaches

Within the region, the attention garnered by these disputes focuses more on the competing claims over sovereignty and economic rights in the sea, than the parallel dispute concerning freedom of navigation. Whilst most countries in the region are broadly supportive of US monitoring of growing Chinese military capabilities – recognising the contribution to regional security that such surveillance activities can make – some are also sympathetic to China's position. After all, they also have to consider a possible future world where the US does withdraw – either voluntarily or under duress – from its position as the primary guarantor of maritime security in Asia. Do these same Southeast Asian countries want Chinese submarines operating freely within their EEZs, gathering information on their inferior capabilities? In these circumstances, it is perhaps unsurprising that China is winning some support for the restrictions it argues it should legally be able to impose on foreign military vessels operating within its EEZ. Even one rival claimant, Malaysia, appears to side with China on this issue.[12] Similarly, when Thailand ratified the UNCLOS treaty in May 2011, article 1.4 of the government's statement of ratification noted its understanding that the treaty did not entitle foreign navies to conduct activities which 'may affect the rights or interests of the coastal state' without the consent of that coastal state.[13]

On sovereignty disputes themselves, the range of attitudes and strategies towards managing the rival claims is as diverse as the assorted claimants involved. At the activist end of the spectrum come Vietnam and the Philippines. Aside from Taiwan, Vietnam's claims overlap with China's to a greater extent than any other claimant. Close geographical proximity and a history of interactions which can at best be described as complicated further helps feed tensions. Meanwhile, the Philippines may have one of the region's least capable militaries but, perversely perhaps, this can actually fuel tensions. One argument goes that, as China is becoming stronger and US staying power appears unclear, the region is facing a strategic window of opportunity for non-Chinese claimants to press their claims. If realities in the changing balance of power are not to result in a de facto convenient recognition of Chinese claims by outside powers, then rival claimants in particular and Southeast Asian states in general need to be more active in addressing the issues rather than 'setting them to one side' as Chinese theory advises. The cautious but deliberate internationalisation of these sovereignty disputes, including to some extent the current push for hydrocarbon exploitation, is therefore a strategic move, perceived as being in in the respective national interests of both the Philippines and Vietnam.

Malaysia and Brunei – the other two claimants who are also members of ASEAN – take a less active approach. Indeed, at times, certain non-claimant members of ASEAN, such as Singapore, appear comparatively more concerned about the management of these disputes. Other ASEAN member states such as Indonesia also have an established record of active engagement with the disputes. Lastly, at the other end of the scale from Vietnam and the Philippines, come those non-claimant members of ASEAN, such as Laos, Myanmar and Cambodia, who are traditionally closer to China and who remain at best ambivalent about the prospect of complicating their own important bilateral relationships with China through unnecessary involvement in the tensions of others.

Naturally, these assorted reactions result from differing threat perceptions about what the rise of China portends for the region, and are magnified by the lack of a clear regional identity or established regional norms. These varying reactions, in turn, give rise to a range of attitudes towards the extent to which it is reasonable to push China on sovereignty issues in the South China Sea. Is, for example, the Philippines right to worry about a strategic window of opportunity or is it instead behaving recklessly, perhaps misguidedly emboldened by the security treaty commitments of its US ally? Similarly, these varying reactions also give rise to a range of attitudes over the extent to which greater engagement by the US military in the region is desirable. The danger is the creation of a vicious circle, whereby the regional security dilemma created by China's rise leads to the development of greater 'balancing' ties with the US, which in turn feeds Chinese insecurity over containment and its narrative of needing to break beyond its island chains. In this scenario, the negative implications for China's approach to the South China Sea disputes in particular, as well as for regional security dynamics in general, are clear.

## Leading the charge – Vietnam and the Philippines

Vietnam and, to a lesser extent, the Philippines are ASEAN's 'front line' in sovereignty disputes in the South China Sea. Tensions with China are more obvious and more politically charged, whilst clashes occur more regularly. A backdrop of blood spilt – both in land wars and at sea – between China and Vietnam adds a further popular emotional tension to discussions on island sovereignty.

As the only ASEAN member also laying claim to the Paracels, Vietnam has to try both to convince China to negotiate over a dispute that Beijing refuses even to recognise, as well as to convince fellow ASEAN members to include the additional complications of the Paracels in their deliberations on sovereignty disputes in the sea. Indeed Vietnam's continued insistence on the inclusion of the Paracels in negotiations undoubtedly proved a further hindrance in its efforts, as chair of ASEAN in 2010, to persuade the organisation to adopt a more activist approach to the disputes. Meanwhile, to Chinese consternation, Vietnamese activism noticeably extended beyond ASEAN to include interested third parties, in particular the US.[14]

Since 2009, the Philippines has been equally ready to allow, and even to attract, an international spotlight on to these disputes, but its attempts to engage ASEAN have likewise met with limited success.[15] In 2011, the Philippines attempted to co-opt ASEAN on its proposal for the creation of a new joint development zone in uncontested waters within the South China Sea, which it called the Zone of Peace, Friendship, and Cooperation. Although ASEAN foreign ministers duly considered the proposal in July of that year, reactions were lukewarm at best. This may have been, in part, because the chances of the zone's realisation were low from the outset. China quickly made its disapproval clear, for example protesting a meeting of ASEAN legal experts examining the proposal.[16]

Similarly, during its stand-off with China at the Scarborough Reef in 2012, the Philippines noticeably failed to attract even a single statement of support by ASEAN. Privately, many in the region, including actors themselves concerned at Chinese behaviour in the South China Sea such as Singapore, worried about misguided Philippine assertiveness.[17] Was it really only an accident of geography that led to the deployment of a warship to arrest Chinese fishermen? Did the Philippines not understand that its overt lobbying for US engagement was in danger of polarising a region anxious to avoid any such choice between its primary trading and security partners? Whilst some ASEAN countries, such as Singapore, appeared to see the regional trend towards renewed enthusiasm for US engagement through 2010–11 as a tactical tool intended to remind Chinese partners of Southeast Asia's alternative diplomatic options, the Philippines seemed ready to view it as a point of departure – a reset of relations, involving new parameters that sanctioned more provocative behaviour.

Meanwhile, repeated patrols by Chinese maritime paramilitary vessels within both countries' claimed EEZs feed a popular narrative of required reaction in the face of Chinese assertiveness. For example, seen from Manila, in the space of a few months in 2011 alone, the Philippines faced: the Reed Bank incident, where two Chinese patrol boats harassed a survey ship conducting seismic studies for the Philippine government within the country's EEZ (March); a PLAN patrol near Amy Douglas Bank (May); allegations of Chinese construction at Amy Douglas Bank (May) and Rajah Soliman Reef (June); and harassment of Filipino fishing vessels at Jackson Atoll (June).[18]

Bilaterally, both Vietnam and the Philippines have proved particularly ready to assert their interests with regard to resources in the South China Sea, where growing domestic requirements are increasing the stakes in the sea's hydrocarbons and fisheries. For example, whilst production from PetroVietnam's established fields has been declining, Vietnam's energy demand is set to triple in the coming ten years, with the country destined to become a net importer of energy around 2015.[19] Furthermore, approximately one-third of Vietnam's population lives along the coast and its maritime industries sector, centring on hydrocarbons and fishing, already accounted for 50% of the country's GDP in 2012 – with this figure only set to rise.[20]

Efforts at collaborative hydrocarbon exploration in the sea between China and Southeast Asia have ground to a halt following the failure of the Joint Marine Seismic Undertaking (JMSU), which began in 2005 and lapsed in 2008 with little to show for any of the participants (China, Vietnam and the Philippines) beyond a diplomatic scandal in Manila. Instead, unilateral actions have been the order of the day. To Beijing, it has appeared as though Vietnam and the Philippines have been developing a resource strategy of unilaterally inviting in international oil companies to explore contested waters, either then to help themselves to resources which China claims, or to use any adverse reactions on the part of China to attract further international attention to the disputes.[21]

Like China, both Vietnam and the Philippines have also been deploying administrative and jurisdictional means to entrench further their claims. In April 2007, Vietnam upgraded Spratly Island to 'township' level under the Truong Sa District, improving administrative capabilities for the region. In February 2009, the Philippine legislature adopted its archipelagic baseline law, covering its claims within the Spratlys.[22] In June 2012, the Vietnamese National Assembly passed a maritime law defining its waters in accordance with UNCLOS, in the process clearly reasserting Vietnamese sovereignty claims over the Paracels and Spratlys.[23]

Again as in China, the population in general and the media in particular are also mobilised in the promotion of rival claims. Moreover, whereas Chinese leaders have refrained from making high-level visits to disputed islands, Vietnamese leaders have not. In March 2010, for example, Vietnamese Prime Minister Nguyen Tan Dung made a public visit to a Vietnamese-held island in the Spratlys, attracting public attention and popular domestic support for Vietnam's territorial claims.[24] Yet some domestic lobbying for Vietnam's sovereignty claims is less welcome. In March and again in October 2010, the dissident pro-democracy group Viet Tan held demonstrations in Hanoi calling for the Vietnamese government to do more to defend the country's sovereignty over the Paracel and Spratly islands.

Yet unlike China, the Philippines has been exploring not just domestic legal options but also international ones. In January 2013, the Philippines announced their intention unilaterally to refer their dispute with China in the South China Sea to an arbitration tribunal under UNCLOS. The submission argued that China's nine-dashed line 'interfered with the lawful exercise by the Philippines of its rights within its legitimate maritime zones', with Foreign Secretary Albert Del Rosario arguing separately that his country had had no alternative; the Philippines had 'exhausted almost all political and diplomatic avenues'.[25] This move by the Philipinnes ignores the fact that the International Tribunal on the Law of the Sea (ITLOS) – the independent judicial body established under UNCLOS to adjudicate disputes under the convention – does not have jurisdiction if both parties do not agree to refer the dispute to the tribunal and China has emphatically rejected such international arbitration.[26] For the moment, the move therefore appears more symbolic than substantive, although any eventual decision in favour of the Philippines would likely have helpful diplomatic benefits in terms of the support the country receives for its position in the international arena. Meanwhile China is left facing a dilemma: participate in a process which will force it to argue the validity of the nine-dashed line and its 'historic rights' before a third party; or shun the process, as it is legally entitled to do, but risk confirming suspicions about its relative disregard for international law.[27]

Lastly, both ASEAN countries have also been investing in improving their own military capabilities. Vietnam, for example, has invested significantly in its navy, ordering from Russia – its primary arms supplier – six *Kilo*-class submarines and four *Gepard*-class frigates. In February 2012, Russia and Vietnam agreed to collaborate on the production of Kh-35U (SS-N-25 *Switchblade*) anti-ship missiles, which will greatly aid Hanoi in supplying its frigates, which each carry eight of these missiles.[28] Vietnam has also not been averse to showcasing its efforts to improve its hard-power capabilities, holding in June 2011, for example, its own live-fire naval exercises in the South China Sea.

Meanwhile, in light of the paucity of equipment currently in its arsenal, the Philippines has been eager to expand its own military, and in particular naval capabilities. Traditionally, the

Philippines has maintained a relatively low level of defence expenditure compared to its GDP, partially owing to its favourable geographical position as an island nation on the outskirts of Asia, as well as to a desire to curtail its military from being able to upset the political process more regularly than it already does. What defence spending there has been had therefore been concentrated on the army and air force, and was particularly focused on combating the national communist and southern Islamist separatist insurgencies that continue to blight areas of the country. However, Manila is slowly changing this situation and focus, approving, for example, a 7.6% increase in its defence budget for 2013, with the extra funds earmarked for bolstering its lacklustre navy.

Nevertheless, the regional disparity between these efforts and the parallel military advancements being made by China remains stark. In 2011, China spent US$137bn on its armed forces according to the IISS's *Military Balance* – more than 50 times as much as the Philippines' budget in 2012.

With these inequalities in mind, both Vietnam and the Philippines have also been reinsuring through the expansion of security ties with the US. Following the launch of a strategic dialogue on security issues with the US in 2008, joint naval exercises between the US and Vietnam began in 2010, although these are limited to noncombat activities and cannot therefore be compared to exercises conducted between the US and other longer-term allies and partners in the region, including the Philippines. Vietnam has also been careful to balance, to some extent, progress in security ties to the 'imperialist' US with developments in its relations with its fellow communist government in China, with whom it now conducts a strategic dialogue at the level of deputy defence minister. And whilst the US may have been first to take advantage of the opening up of commercial repair facilities at Vietnam's naval facility at Cam

Ranh Bay, with the dispatch of three Military Sealift Command ships for minor repairs, Vietnam has opened up these facilities to all nations and navies.[29] At the end of July 2012, for example, Vietnam stated that it would allow Russia to set up a ship maintenance facility at Cam Ranh Bay, and Moscow is already constructing a submarine maintenance facility for Vietnam in the same area.

Meanwhile, military ties between the US and the Philippines are already close: since 2002, the Pentagon has rotated hundreds of troops through the country, while the *Balikatan* exercises, held annually since 1981 save for a four-year hiatus in the mid-1990s, assumed a new significance in the 2000s as the US aimed to focus its efforts on transnational non-state armed groups such as Jemaah Islamiyah and the Abu Sayyaf group. Bilateral military ties were again reaffirmed in the wake of the US 'pivot' to Asia. This was demonstrated symbolically through the Manila Declaration of November 2011 (which reiterated obligations under the 1951 Mutual Defence Treaty), and practically through the donation in 2011 of two former US Coast Guard cutters to the Philippine Navy.

Yet whilst the dynamics of dispute management in recent years have been increasingly negative – including political, resource, bureaucratic, legal, nationalist and military tensions as outlined above – limited progress has been made in some areas between these key rival claimants. For example, in October 2011, Vietnam and China did manage to negotiate bilaterally an agreement covering six basic principles for dispute management at sea, including the establishment of a defence hotline between the two countries. Meanwhile, the broader trend of closer economic integration continues to offer a more positive backdrop. China is now Vietnam's largest trading partner, providing around a quarter of Vietnam's overall imports in 2010 and, in 2011, Vietnam's trade deficit with China was

US$12.7bn. Whilst the dumping of cheap products and the undervaluation of the yuan impact negatively on local manufacturing in Vietnam, as they do across Southeast Asia, China has embedded itself as the necessary constant in the Vietnamese economy. As one former deputy foreign minister commented, 'statistically, we're one province of China'.[30] Meanwhile, China is the Philippines' fastest growing trade partner, and presently third on its list of overall trading partners, but with obvious potential to rise yet higher. Nevertheless, the balance of trade within these interactions is worth noting, as it offers a further reminder of the potential reach and influence of China within Southeast Asian economies.

## The quieter claimants – Malaysia and Brunei

Fellow claimants Malaysia and Brunei have been considerably more reluctant to draw attention to their disputes with China in the South China Sea. Challenges of the Chinese position are therefore rare but not non-existent. For example, in March 2009, then Malaysian Prime Minister Abdullah Ahmad Badawi made a public visit to Malaysian-occupied Swallow Reef in the Spratly Islands in support of his country's territorial claims. Then in May 2009, Malaysia submitted a joint claim with Vietnam to UNCLOS, which resulted in China's reactive protest note that included its first official submission of the nine-dashed line map. Malaysia and Brunei have also been quietly exploiting the sea's resources, with Malaysia in particular extracting substantial resources in deep-water development in areas to which China also lays claim.[31] For example, in June 2011 Malaysia's state-owned hydrocarbons company, Petronas, was operating 13 oil and gas fields in the South China Sea off the eastern coast of the state of Terengganu, and in August 2011 announced a MYR15bn (US$6bn) project to develop further gas fields in the area.[32]

There are a variety of important contextual factors serving to dampen the fall-out from competing claims on Malaysia's and Brunei's respective bilateral relationship with China. These include the reality that there are more important targets of nationalist concern closer to home. For example, Malaysian disputes with Indonesia over maritime sovereignty off the eastern coast of Borneo and areas not yet delimited in the northern section of the Strait of Malacca tend to attract more concern from the general public than disputes with the more geographically distant China. Moreover, in terms of a territorial presence on Malaysian-claimed territory, China is notably absent; only Vietnam and the Philippines actually occupy any of the islands covered under Malaysia's claims in the southern Spratlys.

Despite the history of often-strained relations between the local Chinese community and indigenous Malays, which has intermittently complicated the bilateral relationship, this relatively calmer backdrop with regard to the South China Sea allows the Malaysian government more room to concentrate on the bigger picture of increasing economic interactions with China. China is now Malaysia's largest trade partner. And as China's third-largest trading partner after Japan and South Korea, Malaysia also has more influence with China than most inside ASEAN. Lastly, Malaysia's appreciation for China's contention that military activities and surveillance are not covered by the guarantee to freedom of navigation and over-flight contained within Article 58 of UNCLOS also provides helpful common ground.

Brunei claims two features in the Spratly Islands – the low-tide elevation of Louisa Reef and the entirely submerged Rifleman Bank – and has made a partial submission to the CLCS over an extended continental shelf. However, it occupies no islands and has no military presence in the South China

Sea. While it exchanged letters with Malaysia in 2009 to delimit their maritime boundaries up to 200nm, its island claims and extended continental shelf mean it infringes on the claims of others, including China.[33] Despite this potential source of tension, China has made considerable diplomatic inroads in Brunei since the establishment of diplomatic relations in 1991. This has been overseen in part by a series of high-level visits in recent years, including a visit by Premier Wen Jiabao in 2011 – the first visit in Brunei's history by a modern Chinese premier. Something of a tacit quid pro quo would appear to have been reached between the two countries. Two of Brunei's key deep-water concessions, which are so important for its future wealth and political stability, are in areas claimed by China. Yet China does little to protest these, including when Brunei and Malaysia reached agreement in 2009 over a share of the proceeds from their exploration in disputed territory. In return, Brunei largely respects China's preference for keeping dialogue bilateral rather than multilateral, acting as a brake on ASEAN caucusing of China with regard to the South China Sea. Brunei's role as ASEAN chair in 2013 is set inevitably to force it into a higher-profile role in the regional management of these disputes than it has traditionally sought, presenting it with a considerable diplomatic challenge. Yet China appears well aware of this potential dilemma, and anxious to help Brunei offset it, with Foreign Minister Yang Jiechi stressing in early 2013 China's interests in 'upgrading the China-Brunei cooperation'.[34]

## Anxious ASEAN – Indonesia, Singapore and Thailand

Historically, Indonesia has demonstrated perhaps the most active interest of all non-claimants in dispute management in the sea, in part because of its particular investments in ASEAN as a founding member and its ongoing role as host of the

ASEAN general secretariat. Beginning in 1990, it has hosted an annual non-official workshop on managing potential conflicts in the South China Sea, keeping discussions of these challenges alive through times when the disputes were attracting little international attention and when the process of dispute management within the region had largely stalled. Indonesia was instrumental as chair of ASEAN in the signing of the guidelines in 2011, and has been similarly active in the pursuit of a meaningful code of conduct.[35] In 2012, Indonesia's role as a broker within ASEAN was again tested by the failure of the annual meeting of ASEAN foreign ministers to issue a final communiqué, for the first time in its 45-year history, reflecting pressure from Vietnam and the Philippines to address recent clashes in the sea and concern from others, most notably Cambodia, to avoid any such reference. Where only a month earlier at the 2012 Shangri-La Dialogue, Indonesian President Susilo Bambang Yudhoyono had been talking about ushering in 'the geopolitics of cooperation', Indonesian Foreign Minister Marty Natalegawa now quickly suggested that some ASEAN members had acted 'irresponsibly'.[36] Nevertheless, it was Natalegawa who undertook the shuttle diplomacy required to help shore up ASEAN credibility, quickly visiting five Southeast Asian capitals to deliver a face-saving agreement on 'Six Point Principles on the South China Sea'. Whilst this agreement signalled a return to 'business as usual', as Natalegawa claimed, perhaps only in so much as the Six Points were rather light on substance, Indonesia once again proved itself the catalyst for papering over – if not quite overcoming – ASEAN disunity.[37]

Of course, not all of Indonesia's interests in the disputes stem from its investments in ASEAN. It also has its own concerns about the meaning of China's nine-dashed line, including a potential conflict with Indonesia's own claims north and east of the Natuna Islands, which host one of Asia's largest concentrations of natural-gas reserves.[38] In May 2012, the regional military commander with responsibility for the Natunas declared an 'urgent' need to boost Indonesian troops posted to the region, in order 'to maintain the sovereignty and integrity of Indonesia'.[39] Clashes have occurred, most notably in June 2010 when an Indonesian patrol boat arrested Chinese trawlers allegedly fishing illegally in Natuna's waters and was confronted by a Chinese maritime constabulary vessel. Indonesia has also publicly challenged Beijing's position in the form of a July 2010 diplomatic note to the UN noting that Chinese claims have 'no clear explanation as to the legal basis' and 'is tantamount to upset the UNCLOS 1982.'[40] The country also has rival hydrocarbon interests, with its national oil company, Pertamina, partnering in 2002 with Malaysia's Petronas and Vietnam's PetroVietnam to explore for oil in blocks 10 and 11.1 of the Nam Con Son Basin, parts of which are located within China's claims.[41] Meanwhile, it has also been following its own programme of military modernisation, with naval plans from the Ministry of Defence focused, according to the concept of 'minimum essential forces', on the development of 'green water capabilities' by 2024 capable of protecting key sea lanes from external threats.[42]

Yet despite these points of tension with regard to the Sea, bilateral relations between Indonesia and China are generally positive. Trade in 2011 stood at about US$66obn. Interactions range from mining to agriculture and from hydroelectric generation to textile manufacturing. In April 2011, during a visit by Premier Wen Jiabao to Jakarta, China pledged US$19bn in investment credit to Indonesia, including US$9bn loans for infrastructure development.[43] Even in the field of military modernisation, where Indonesia's motivations may be partially attributed to China's own impressive programme of naval development, there is clear cooperation. Since 2008, Indonesia has acquired C-802 anti-ship missiles, whilst negotiations began in July 2012 to reach an agreement by March 2013 on the production of Chinese-designed C-705 anti-ship missiles in Indonesia.

Singapore has been less proactive in public about the need for responsible dispute management in the South China Sea, but behind the scenes it has been no less concerned, leading the way, for example, in raising the South China Sea at the 2012 EAS against Chinese wishes. It has also been vocal in demanding that China clarify its claims, as the 'current ambiguity as to their extent has caused significant concerns in the international maritime community'.[44] As a major trading port, Singapore has obvious financial as well as security interests wrapped up in the freedom and safety of sea lines of communication in the South China Sea. Interestingly, the public airing of Singapore's demand for clarification came in the wake of Singaporean frustration at Chinese behaviour following the docking of Chinese Maritime Safety Administration patrol vessel, *Haixun 31*, in Singapore in June 2011. What had been presented to Singapore as a friendly port call at the end of the vessel's journey through the South China Sea was reported in China's *People's Daily*, as having been a considerably more provocative check on 'oil rigs, stationary ships' operations in constructions and surveys … and … on foreign ships navigating, anchored and operating in Chinese waters'.[45]

Thailand's position within this category of 'anxious actors' is perhaps the most tenuous. It does not hold a claim in the South China Sea, but as an original member of ASEAN, a current disputant with Cambodia in the Gulf of Thailand and the architect of joint development areas in the gulf with Malaysia and Vietnam, it has both interest in and experience of regional maritime disputes. However, Thailand also serves as a clear

example of a Southeast Asian state moving to balance its relations with both the US and China, whilst taking Washington's
declining relative influence since the end of the Cold War into
consideration. Certainly, as coordinating country for relations
between ASEAN and China from July 2012–2015, Beijing has
been making considerable efforts on a bilateral basis to allay
Thai apprehensions surrounding the sea. Sino-Thai cooperation has been duly lauded in China as an example for other
ASEAN nations to follow.[46]

Yet whilst Thailand was the first ASEAN country to establish
a strategic partnership with China and to hold joint military
exercises, trade is once more the centrepiece of the relationship. China is Thailand's second-largest trading partner, with
trade standing at US$64.74bn in 2011. Meanwhile, a record
1.76 million Chinese tourists visited Thailand in 2011, a 60%
increase on 2010.[47] Nevertheless, security ties are also increasingly in evidence. In spring 2012, a Thai delegation headed
by Defence Minister Sukhupol Suwannathat, and including
Army Commander in Chief Gen Prayuth Chan-ocha visited
Beijing for defence talks that covered the South China Sea.
Thailand is also developing its own naval capabilities, notably
purchasing former Chinese Type 053 frigates to complement
its two-vessel *Naresuan*-class and also buying two *Pattani*-class
corvettes, which bear some resemblance to China's new Type
056 corvette that it started mass producing at an impressive
rate in 2012.

## Disinterested ASEAN – Cambodia, Myanmar, Laos
Other states within ASEAN hold a less active interest in the
South China Sea disputes for two reasons: firstly, they hold no
direct claims in the sea; and, secondly, they are close allies of
China, which usually discourages non-claimants from involve-
ment in the disputes.

Cambodia's ambivalence towards too active an involvement in the South China Sea disputes was clearly highlighted during its chairmanship of ASEAN in 2012. After two years of rotating chairs in Vietnam and then Indonesia, where both were ready to allow and even push these disputes onto the ASEAN agenda, Cambodia's approach as chair was marked with what can best be interpreted as obvious disinterest. The failure to issue a final communiqué at the annual foreign ministers' meeting in Phnom Penh reflected not only the discord within ASEAN on issues surrounding the South China Sea, but also Cambodia's particular ambivalence about attempting to work through these issues.[48]

China's cultivation of Cambodia appears to be paying political dividends. Indeed, shortly before Cambodia hosted the annual summit, Chinese President Hu Jintao flew to Phnom Penh. His four-day visit was the first visit by a Chinese head of state to Cambodia in more than 12 years. During the visit (declared a 'complete success' in the subsequent joint statement), China pledged almost US$40m in grants and more than US$30m in loans.[49] Subsequently, China agreed seven loan agreements worth US$500m and a US$24m grant to Cambodia during another trip by Prime Minister Hun Sen to China in September 2012.[50] As Sam Rainsy Party lawmaker Son Chhay argued disapprovingly, 'It's a move away from the neutrality that Cambodia is supposed to support as a country. By giving so many loans, China is able to control Cambodia's policy.'[51] Meanwhile, Prime Minister Hun Sen reassured Chinese President Hu Jintao that Cambodia shares China's belief that disputes in the South China Sea should not be 'internationalised'.[52] In a naked sign of agreement that Beijing's influence was being felt in Cambodia's role as ASEAN chair, according to Chinese state-owned news agency Xinhua, Chinese Legal Affairs Committee President Hu Kangsheng thanked

Cambodia's National Assembly President Heng Samrin in December 2012 for 'its staunch support ... on issues related to China's core interests'.[53]

Expanding economic interactions are bringing their own political consequences as well. Between 1994 and 2011, China invested US$8.8bn in Cambodia, making it the largest investor in a country where it also likely the biggest aid donor.[54] In 2011 alone, Phnom Penh received ten times more in foreign invest-ment pledges from China than from the US.[55] As one adviser to the King of Cambodia explained to the authors in mid-2012, China understood how to help Cambodia as a partner at a time when others understood only how to treat it as an infe-rior recipient of aid. Cambodia simply has no national interest in alienating such an important partner for the sake of a third party, nor does it wish to facilitate others trying to play a complicated and potentially dangerous game through the encouragement of US involvement in these disputes.[56]

Similarly, Myanmar and Laos have traditionally also had little to say on the disputes. Historically, economically and politically closer to China, there is little immediate incentive for these disputes to make it on to their respective foreign-policy agendas.

## The peculiar position of Taiwan

While China and Taiwan maintain all but identical claims, dynamics are complicated by their contradictory opinions on which 'China' it is that in fact has sovereignty over these islands. Given that it effectively sees Taipei's claims as its own, Beijing does little to complain about them, or indeed Taiwan's occupation of the Pratas Islands and Itu Aba Island – the largest of the Spratly Islands. Indeed, it has even made some outreach on joint action in fields such as hydrocarbon exploration and maritime patrols.[57] Nevertheless, it does continuously attempt to limit the opportunities in which Taiwan can press these claims as an independent actor. Taiwan is not party to ASEAN discussions or a signatory to UNCLOS, and has limited opportunities for bilateral discussions with other actors, given that it has no diplomatic relations with these claimants. On the one hand, these rival claimants lobby Taiwan not to work bilaterally with China on these disputes; on the other, they themselves find it difficult to engage with Taiwan as a result of pressure from China on both Taiwan and these rival claimants.

Nevertheless, Taiwan has been far from immune to rising friction in the South China Sea. Tensions with Vietnam have been particularly noticeable, with Taiwanese law-makers claiming a total of 106 Vietnamese incursions into Taiwan's territorial seas around Taiping Island in 2011 alone.[58] Indeed, there have been some in Taiwan pointing to the advantages of protective cover from the PLA against the designs of Manila or Hanoi, with these island disputes thereby serving to support rather than undermine the argument for cross-straits cooperation.[59] In the meantime however, hard-power reinforcements have been made in the area, alongside high-profile, high-level visits to demonstrate sovereignty, including for example Chen Shui-bian in 2009 to Itu Aba. While Taiwan has set about establishing an 'airborne unit for the Spratlys', after completing a runway on the island in 2008, its permanent deployment remains limited to approximately 200 coast-guard personnel armed with small arms, mortars and anti-aircraft guns.[60]

## Working together within ASEAN?

Given the diversity of regional perspectives regarding the meaning of China's rise, as well as concerning the relevant actors and their respective roles in dispute management in the South China Sea, it is no surprise that this sea has served both to highlight and fuel tensions within ASEAN. Following the golden years of relative stability around the time of the signing of the DoC in 2002, there have been further moments of ASEAN convergence, in particular when more assertive behaviour on the part of China has encouraged members to look at the broader strategic picture beyond their own internal squabbles. Indeed, throughout 2010, Vietnam sought, with a modicum of success, to harness diverse regional experiences of Chinese assertiveness to create an ASEAN-centred but internationalised discussion of these concerns. Yet any such limited successes have proved short lived against a backdrop of differing threat assessments of the ambition, prospect and consequence of Chinese ambitions in the South China Sea.

The lines of disagreement are clear. What format or grouping is most appropriate for discussing these disputes? To what degree should other interested parties beyond ASEAN, in particular the US, be invited to become involved? At what point should China be engaged in discussions, for example on a Code of Conduct? And how should ASEAN react when China stalls?

Weak statements by ASEAN on the disputes have therefore become something of the norm. But, whilst foreign ministers were able to agree on the 'key elements' in a future Code of Conduct during their ministerial meeting of July 2012, the failure to find sufficient common ground for a final communiqué at this same meeting caught even those established sceptics of ASEAN's ability to manage these disputes by surprise.[61] As Cambodia and the Philippines resorted to blaming each other for this failure, and Singapore's foreign minister labelled it a 'severe dent' in the credibility of ASEAN, all could agree that it did little to demonstrate ASEAN's slogan, 'One Community, One Destiny'.[62] Cracks in the facade once again appeared at the EAS heads of state meeting in November 2012, when a briefing by the summit's Cambodian hosts that ASEAN participants had reached agreement 'not to internationalise the [South China Sea] issue' was publicly criticised and corrected by Philippine President Benigno Aquino III, who commented tersely, 'There were several views expressed yesterday on ASEAN unity which we did not realise would be translated into an ASEAN consensus.'[63]

How significant a break the July 2012 blockage and November 2012 diplomatic fracas were in ASEAN's culture of consensus remains to be seen. The question of whether big-power rivalry will highlight the clear divides that already exist within ASEAN, despite ASEAN intentions to the contrary, similarly remains unanswered as yet. Certainly, in the same way that the 2002 DoC was as much a reflection as a precipitator of improved China–ASEAN relations, so the difficulties encountered in negotiating a Code of Conduct have both reflected and fuelled underlying mistrust and rivalry.

Other regional forums also offer opportunities for discussions on maritime security, including the South China Sea. There is the established and increasingly important EAS – comprising of the ten states of ASEAN plus Australia, China, India, Japan, New Zealand, Russia, South Korea and the US. Then there is the yet broader membership of the ASEAN Regional Forum (ARF). More recently, in October 2010, Vietnam hosted the inaugural meeting of ASEAN defence ministers with eight key dialogue partners, including the US. Known as the ADMM Plus, the objective is to build confidence and connections between the region's armed forces. Although still immature in its impact, this body has at least established an expert working group focused on maritime security which meets twice a year to consider initiatives for practical cooperation in the South China Sea.

The danger, however, of too many organisations operating under the auspices of ASEAN, all with overlapping responsibilities and therefore only limited accountability, remains – both in terms of broader maritime security issues as well as the management of specific tensions within the South China Sea. With other forums involved even within ASEAN, including for example the ASEAN Maritime Forum and the ASEAN Navy Chiefs Meeting, the fear is that quantity is making up for quality. Indeed, the third iteration of the ASEAN Maritime Forum, held in October 2012 in Manila, only reinforced this possibility, immediately followed as it was by the inaugural Expanded ASEAN Maritime Forum, an enlarged group that included the ASEAN members as well as Australia, China, India, Japan, New Zealand, South Korea Russia and the US. Whilst greater scrutiny of the issues at stake is certainly welcomed and whilst this forum could yet provide a useful meeting point for interested parties and encourage multilateral discussions, the risk remains that, without clear lines of responsibility and accountability, the proliferation of meetings around the South China Sea will only reiterate, or worse dilute, discussion on the key issues.

## Distrust in defence

The underlying regional tensions which continue to combine to help thwart the emergence of a powerful regional actor in ASEAN are perhaps most in evidence in the respective defence strategies and procurement purchases of its member states. Although China looms large in the thinking of all members, it does not always loom first; mistrust between ASEAN member states continues to influence the region's ongoing military modernisation.

One area where the overlap between the influence of China and sub-regional dynamics can be clearly seen has been in the recent flurry of submarine purchases throughout Southeast Asia. For whilst it could be argued that Southeast Asian states are purchasing submarines simply to be able to provide a broader spectrum of capabilities, it is difficult to detach these purchases from the notion that these states increasingly perceive a requirement for an asymmetric sea-denial capability to challenge China's growing dominance of the sea. After all, submarines remain the pre-eminent sea-denial capability: while the most expensive form of naval vessel on a per-tonne basis, they have an excellent force-multiplier effect as just one submarine is capable of seeding doubt in a rival over a large area of water. Mobile and difficult to track, a submarine retains one of the most useful of factors in a military engagement: surprise. It is, for example, of more than technical interest that the submarine purchases made over the past decade by Southeast Asian states will all incorporate Air-Independent Propulsion (AIP), a technology that negates the need for submarines to snorkel for oxygen frequently and therefore enables them to patrol submerged for up to three weeks at a time. This significantly enhances the ability of these submarines to act as a surprise weapon, as the longer they are submerged the more difficult it is to track them.

Little wonder, then, that Southeast Asian states have been eager to procure these boats. Vietnam has been at the forefront of this trend, ordering six *Kilo*-class submarines from Russia, with the first launched in August 2012. Having previously only operated midget submarines, this effectively provides Hanoi for the first time with a viable, regional submarine capability. The purchase can be explained largely by its fear of China. The growth in numbers and sophistication of China's surface fleet means the Vietnamese People's Navy is heavily outmatched by the PLAN.

For another new entrant into the submarine-operations market, Malaysia, motivations are less clear-cut. Given its lack of direct naval rivalry with China, the commission in 2009 of two *Scorpène* submarines from France appears to be inspired more by Singapore's status as a submarine operator. Between 1995 and 1997, Singapore purchased four *Challenger*-class submarines (former *Sjöormen*-class) from Sweden. In 2005 it purchased a further two boats – former Swedish *Västergötland* submarines to replace two of the *Challenger*-class, as a new *Archer* class that includes AIP.

Other Southeast Asian states are also pursuing AIP-equipped submarine programmes, furthering the idea that this is a regional trend, fuelled by state-based rivalries and competitions, to bolster naval capabilities in the face of uncertainties over regional stability, including with regard to the South China Sea. Indonesia, for example, signed a contract with Daewoo Shipbuilding and Marine Engineering in December 2011 for the construction of three *Chang Bogo*-class submarines (variants of the German Type 209/1200 design) with the intention of bolstering the two Type 209s (*Cakra*-class) boats they currently have in service. Meanwhile, the Royal Thai Navy has also outlined its desire for a submarine capability, although rumours of a plan to purchase four retired German Type 206A boats (that were started by a *Jane's Defence Weekly* article in March 2011)[64] were proven premature when in February 2012 Bangkok decided to let the option rights expire. Even the Philippines has outlined its desire to procure three submarines by 2020, although whether it has the necessary funds and expertise remains to be seen.[65]

While Taiwan's motivations are more immediately focused on tense cross-strait relations, it too has shown a keen interest in purchasing new submarines: its four boats currently in service are ageing rapidly, with half of them dating to the Second World War. Yet its submarine procurement has been hampered by three factors: a dearth of indigenous shipbuilding expertise, an aversion among European submarine producers to sell to Taiwan to preserve their relationship with China and a total lack of diesel-electric submarine production capabilities in the US (all US Navy submarines are nuclear-powered). To remedy this, Taiwan is currently examining the possibility of indigenous construction of a modest submarine based on a foreign design.[66]

However, submarines are not the only equipment being purchased throughout the region that point to the various insecurities and mistrust existing amongst and between the states of Southeast Asia, as well as China, and that hold potential relevance to the balance of power in the South China Sea disputes. Surface vessels are also becoming more sophisticated and better armed. Vietnam's new *Gepard*-class frigates are designed to protect its EEZs – which is also the focus of the Philippines's naval modernisation. Although thus far restricted to two US-donated former coast-guard cutters, the Philippines's procurement will likely concentrate in future on offshore patrol vessels and fast attack craft. Indonesia's procurement of SIGMA-class frigates and KCR-40 fast attack craft is similarly aimed at securing its territorial and economic waters.

Meanwhile, these purchases are being supported by the proliferation of more capable, ship-based anti-ship missiles throughout the region, whether involving the sale of Chinese C-802 and C-705 missiles to Indonesia or Kh-35U missiles to Vietnam. The Philippine Department of Defence also noted in January 2012 that it was considering the purchase of such missiles for the first time, which, given the difficulty in destroying them in flight and the potential damage just one round can do, act as an effective asymmetric capability. Ironically, just as small Southeast Asian states purchase them as defence against an increasingly dominant Chinese navy, so the PLAN has deployed anti-ship missiles in significant numbers to counter the US and Japan's large, technologically superior vessels.[67] While the Philippines and Vietnam can point to their worries about an increasingly dominant Chinese navy in the South China Sea to justify their purchases, the Indonesian anti-ship missile development may be better described as an attempt by a maritime country to modernise an insufficient navy amid rapid regional military developments.

Aerial capabilities are a final area worth highlighting as reflective of intra-regional tensions. Malaysia is currently holding a competition for new combat aircraft to replace its MiG-29s; it already operates 18 modern Su-30MKM multirole aircraft. Such aircraft are of limited utility in counter-insurgency operations, and suggest inter-state rivalry, which may reflect the fact that Singapore maintains a very capable fleet of US-produced aircraft (F-15SG, F-16 Block C/D and F-5S/T aircraft) that can only be designed to deter and repel a state-based rival. Malaysia's Su-30MKMs were purchased in 2003, after the Royal Thai Air Force underwent a significant expansion in its own capabilities through the procurement of F-16 A/B aircraft in the 1990s and early 2000s, and also followed Singapore in the purchase of 40 F-16 C/Ds.

Such seemingly reactive dynamics in arms purchases, in both the naval and aerial domains, certainly suggest bilateral rivalry in procurement. For some countries, this may be motivated by the rise of China and growing concern over its perceived assertiveness. For others, such as Malaysia, it may be sub-regional dynamics built on traditional mistrust despite a façade of ASEAN unity and amity. Both of these undercurrents thereby create a region-wide trend that encourages other states to maintain pace with modernisation occurring in their neighbourhood, and so result in a broad, regional defence-modernisation process. While this is difficult to classify definitively as an arms race, given the multiple and sometimes overlapping reasons for the purchases and the fact that the pace of purchases and defence-spending increases do not suggest panic among the participants, it certainly suggests bilateral and multilateral layers of mistrust.

For the South China Sea, this means that, even though maritime paramilitaries are the primary tool of choice in effecting diplomacy, states are also hedging by developing their military capabilities. The result is an increasingly militarised region and a demonstration of the level of distrust among ASEAN states that undermines their ability to collaborate diplomatically in the presentation of a united front in negotiations with China.

## Engaging other third-party interests

Whilst the particular interests and approaches of the US will form the focus of the next chapter, there are, of course, other key user-states of the South China Sea who hold their own interests in the responsible management of tensions there. They too are concerned about the regional implications of a China that is becoming both militarily and economically more powerful. In the context of these sovereignty disputes, they also see their interests as best protected by an insistence on a peaceful approach to dispute resolution and its grounding in international law.

Anxious to broaden the backdrop from one focused on US–China relations, to one centred more around international interests and norms, Southeast Asian nations – led by Vietnam, the Philippines, Singapore and Indonesia as described above – have largely been encouraging such third-party interests. Indeed, the small city-state of Singapore has long followed such an inclusive strategy, working for example during the Cold War to develop close trading ties with Japan and China as well as the US and the USSR.[68] In recent years, Singapore has continued this outreach, including through its assiduous cultivation of India with whom it has developed a bilateral security dialogue aimed at encouraging its Indian colleagues to engage more strategically in the region. The basic strategy appears to be that stability and security comes first and foremost from a continued US military presence, but also from a greater diversity of supporting sources for strategic and economic stability, including on issues concerning the South China Sea.

Japan and South Korea offer fertile ground for such approaches. Both are keenly aware of the strategic importance of the sea for their trade, and in particular for the imported energy on which they depend. As Japan's Foreign Minister Takeaki Matsumoto argued in 2011, 'Japan has a great interest in the territorial disputes in the South China Sea because they could have an impact on peace and security of the Asia-Pacific region, and they are also closely related to safeguarding the security of maritime traffic'.[69] Both countries also have their own island disputes with China to manage; indications of Chinese approaches and thinking to such sovereignty disputes can be garnered from tracking China's behaviour in the South China Sea as well as the East China Sea. Indeed, for Tokyo, the deteriorating bilateral relationship through 2012 over the issue of the Senkaku/Diaoyu Islands in the East China Sea was a matter for particular concern, and served to some extent to motivate a shift in defence posture that includes a rebalance of Japanese forces towards the south of its archipelago and the planned purchase of two further helicopter carriers and submarines. Meanwhile, China's position on the Japanese-controlled Okinotorishima in the Pacific Ocean – where it claims that Okinotorishima is a rock under the definitions provided by UNCLOS Article 121 – and its consequent denial of Japan's claim to an EEZ stemming from this feature (a claim supported by South Korea), is arguably inconsistent with Beijing's equivalent claims resultant from land features in the South China Sea.

Both Japan and South Korea are also paying close attention to the bigger picture of US–China relations around the South China Sea. Japan's security strategy is built on a premise of US regional primacy. If that looks like shifting – and a challenge to this primacy in the South China Sea at least appears credible – then the implications for Japanese and Korean strategic thinkers will be severe.

Guided in part by this concern over the durability of a strong US military presence in Asia, Japan has also responded to Southeast Asia's open door policy by cultivating security ties within the region. Tokyo was integral to the creation of the Regional Cooperation Agreement on Combating Piracy and Armed Robbery (ReCAAP) in 2004, which resulted in a regional information-sharing centre designed to improve counter-piracy efforts in Southeast Asia, and in particular the Straits of Malacca and Singapore. Japan's role in ReCAAP, and other collaborative efforts such as the North Pacific Coast Guard Forum initiated by Tokyo in 2000, is indicative of the country's broader strategic interests in securing its sea lines of communication and maritime security.

In September 2011, during the state visit of the Philippine President to Japan, Tokyo announced that it would be coordinating more closely with all Southeast Asian countries on the South China Sea and the issue of freedom of navigation. An increase in bilateral defence engagement between Japan and the Philippines was duly announced, including a programme of enhanced cooperation between the two countries' respective coast guards and navies, and the supply of coast-guard vessels to Manila to support its attempts to secure its EEZ.[70] (This was followed up in January 2013 with the announcement of an agreement for the Japanese government to provide the Philippines with ten multi-role response vessels along with communications equipment, aimed at boosting Philippine patrol capabilities in the South China Sea.)[71] In an October 2011 visit by Japan's foreign minister to Singapore, Malaysia and Indonesia, the South China Sea was again a key focal point for discussions. The same month, Vietnamese and Japanese defence ministers signed a 'Memorandum on bilateral defence cooperation and exchanges'. When Japanese and Singaporean foreign ministers met in Tokyo in June 2012, a further agreement to strengthen maritime security cooperation was forged. This attention to the region does not appear to be on the wane: the first overseas visit by new Japanese Prime Minister Shinzo Abe in January 2013 was to Southeast Asia (specifically Vietnam, Thailand and Indonesia).[72]

South Korea has also been bolstering its security cooperation, and markets, within the region. In January 2013, for example, it was announced that the Philippines would purchase 12 FA-50 fighter jets from South Korea. Philippine Air Force spokesman Colonel Miguel Ernesto Okol commented, '[these aircraft] will allow us to protect our territories from intruders and their commissioning in Philippines service will greatly boost our external defence capabilities'.[73]

In contrast, India's 'look east' policy has long been more a paper exercise than a reality. However, again with encouragement from ASEAN, signs of a more effective engagement to its east are perhaps, belatedly, beginning to emerge. India has been actively developing its defence ties in the region, for example with Singapore. In 2007, with the establishment of a five-year lease on Kalaikunda airbase in West Bengal, Singapore became the first foreign country to be allowed to lease an Indian military installation on a long-term basis (a subsequent agreement in August 2008 allowed Singapore to deploy personnel for up to eight weeks twice a year to Babina and Deolali ranges for artillery and tank training for five years).[74] Since 2009, India has also hosted an annual Delhi Dialogue to promote cooperation between India and ASEAN. It is actively financing the development of an ASEAN community, including the promotion of infrastructure projects to link ASEAN countries to Indian markets. With the decision, in October 2011, by Indian multinational Oil and Natural Gas Corporation Limited (ONGC) to enter into partnership with PetroVietnam to explore for oil in disputed waters off the Vietnamese coast (following the award of two exploration blocks, 127 and 128, in the Nam Con Son Basin to the Indian company in 2006), India also has direct commercial interests at stake in the South China Sea. Unsurprisingly, this particular venture attracted negative comment in China, with the president of the government-funded National Institute for South China Sea Studies warning that India will face 'political and economic risks' should its companies chose to continue explorations in disputed waters.[75] The Indian navy has also attracted Chinese attention as it has gone about boosting its naval diplomacy in the region. In June 2012, the INS *Shivalik*, one of four Indian navy ships sailing from a port call in the Philippines to one in South Korea, found itself the unexpected beneficiary of a PLAN escort.[76] Although there was nothing overtly aggressive about the service provided by the Chinese frigate, the underlying message of Chinese sovereignty was clear.

Australia has also been paying closer attention to the South China Sea disputes as it monitors the rise of Chinese naval power and supports the continuing presence of the US military as the primary power in the region, including through the basing of US marines on a rotational basis in Darwin. As Australian Foreign Minister Bob Carr noted in a speech in mid-2012, 'Our national interest is to ensure the great success story of this century, the Asian economic transformation, is not distracted by strategic competition in the South China Sea'.[77] Such a 'distraction' would threaten trade flows within the region as well as the regional balance of power – both likely to Australia's detriment.

Russia, meanwhile, has been reinvigorating its relations in Southeast Asia as well, although its interest is driven more by the region's increased procurement activities than a desire for greater strategic engagement, including in the disputes of the South China Sea. Nevertheless, it is playing a key role in the build-up of Vietnamese defence capabilities, for example through the sale of *Kilo*-class submarines already noted, the upgrading of naval facilities at the deep-water port of Cam Ranh Bay, including the construction of a submarine maintenance facility for the navy's new *Kilos*, and a joint venture for oil exploration off Vung Tau. As it once again attempts to reassert a wider global presence, it also appears to be interested in developing relationships that might allow for facilities to station maintenance or supply facilities for Russian naval vessels. In Vietnam's case, this looks to be bearing fruit.[78]

From even further afield, the EU is also beginning to pay attention, as witnessed, for example, in the 2012 EU East Asia Policy Guidelines.[79] Individually, the UK has led the way in pushing for a more robust EU response. It has also been expanding its own bilateralism in the region, for example with Vietnam and the Philippines, as well as increasing its engagement in the Five Powers Defence Arrangements.[80] Yet the reality is that European involvement in the South China Sea dispute remains peripheral, with any possibility of the EU acting as an independent broker limited not least by China's desire to eschew third-party involvement.

ASEAN outreach to third-parties is, of course, far from exclusively focused on military matters. Economic diplomacy and integration remains an important part of the region's security strategy. To this end, alongside the push for a Trans-Pacific Partnership (TPP) that focuses on US engagement in the region (discussed in the next chapter), in November 2012 participants in the EAS agreed, at ASEAN's initiative, to the launch of a Regional Comprehensive Economic Partnership (RCEP). This has the long-term ambition of further integrating Asia's major economies as one cohesive dynamo for growth. Moreover, unlike the TPP, there is no role for the US in the nascent RCEP, whilst there is a role for China – likely even a dominant one, given the sheer size of the country's economy.[81]

## Southeast Asia's role in evolving great-power dynamics

Ultimately, the forces that will shape the balance of great-power relations in Asia in the twenty-first century are varied and complex. Southeast Asian nations, small by comparison though they may be, should not be written off as the inevitable and powerless hosts of great-power competition or condominium. Indeed, it is in part from a recognition that that they will be unlikely to be able to insulate themselves from the broader evolution of great-power relations in Asia, that the smaller and medium-sized powers of Southeast Asia are looking – to differing degrees and with differing capacities – for strategies that enmesh the inevitable interests of these outside powers in the region in ways that enhance rather than undermine regional stability, whilst also protecting their own regional autonomy.

The big geopolitical backdrop to the South China Sea disputes may well be the evolution of relations between China and the US, but the relationships that Southeast Asian nations choose to cultivate with both China and the US will be key influencing factors on this bigger picture and the determination of an evolving regional order. And in its pursuit of a stable neighbourhood policy in Southeast Asia, it is clear that the South China Sea disputes remain China's biggest stumbling block.

## Notes

1  John David Ciorciari 'The Balance of Great-power Influence in Contemporary Southeast Asia', *International Relations of the Asia-Pacific*, vol. 9, 2009, p. 159

2  Amitav Acharya, 'Will Asia's Past be its Future?', *International Security*, vol. 28, no. 3, pp. 150–60.

3  Ciorciari, 'The Balance of Great-power Influence in Contemporary Southeast Asia', p. 163. Quoting Robert Ross: 'The Geography of the peace: East Asia in the Twenty-first Century', *International Security*, vol. 23, no. 4, pp. 81–118.

4  'New U.S. Base in RI's Backyard', *Jakarta Post*, 17 November 2011.

5  For example, Myanmar, Cambodia, Thailand and Laos all have modest defence cooperation with China. Meanwhile, the Philippines and Thailand are both formal allies of the US, yet their security engagement with the US lags that of partners such as Singapore, which hosts military facilities and equipment for US forces. It should also be noted that Thailand hosts *Cobra Gold*, the largest military exercise in the region in which US forces are involved.

6  For the full text of the declaration, see: http://cil.nus.edu.sg/rp/pdf/1971%20Zone%20of%20Peace%20Freedom%20and%20Neutrality%20Declaration-pdf.pdf

7  Lee Kuan Yew, Speech to the Nixon Center, Washington DC, 11 November 1996. Referenced in Eveyln Goh, 'Singapore and the United States: Cooperation on Transnational Security Threats', Paper prepared for 26th Annual Pacific Symposium, Honolulu, Hawaii, 8–10 June 2005, p. 5, http://www.dtic.mil/dtic/tr/fulltext/u2/a441177.pdf.

8  See, for example, Aaron Friedberg, 'Ripe for Rivalry: Prospects for Peace in a Multipolar Asia', *International Security*, vol. 18, no. 3, Winter 1993/94, pp. 5–33.

9  For more detail on aspects of this argument see Evelyn Goh, 'Great Powers and Southeast Asian Regional Security Strategies: Omni-enmeshment, Balancing, and Hierarchical Order', Working Paper No. 84, Institute of Defence and Strategic Studies, July 2005.

10  Ciorciari, 'The Balance of Great-power Influence in Contemporary Southeast Asia', p. 176.

11  This was most obvious in the actions of rival claimants Vietnam and the Philippines, but also in the behaviour of concerned observers such as Singapore.

12  Valencia, 'Foreign Military Activities in Asian EEZs: Conflict Ahead?', National Bureau of Asian Research, Special Report no. 27, May 2011, p. 3.

13  Notification of the Government of the Kingdom of Thailand's Ratification of the United Nations Convention on the Law of the Sea, May 15, 2011. Available at: http://treaties.un.org/doc/Publication/CN/2011/CN.291.2011-Eng.pdf.

14  Indonesia broadly continued with this strategy through its chairmanship in 2011.

15  This coincides with a general upturn in tension in the sea, caused by a range of factors, including the May submission deadline for

claims to an extended continental shelf under UNCLOS. Philippine preparedness to confront China on competing sovereignty disputes seems further to have increased following the election of President Benigno Aquino III in 2010. In 2011, Aquino announced a policy of 'what is ours is ours', indicating that the country would not hold back from exercising its sovereign rights within its EEZ, including with regard to both fisheries and hydrocarbon exploitation.

[16] Ian Storey, 'China's Bilateral and Multilateral Diplomacy in the South China Sea', in Cronin (ed.), *Cooperation from Strength*, p. 60.

[17] Interviews with Cambodian government adviser and Singaporean academic, Shangri-La Dialogue, 2 June 2012.

[18] According to Philippine Armed Forces Deputy Chief of Staff for Intelligence, Major-General Francisco Cruz, quoted in: Rene Acosta, 'Military's Chief Spy Pushes Security Policy for Spratlys', *Business Mirror*, 12 March 2012.

[19] This has complicated implications for Vietnam's relations with China. Vietnam already imports hydroelectricity from China and is dependent on China (and Laos) for maintaining river flow into Vietnam's hydro-power plants.

[20] Kaplan, 'The Vietnam Solution'.

[21] Interview at Chinese Foreign Affairs University, Beijing, 22 September 2009.

[22] The bill was signed into law by the president the following month (in March 2009).

[23] 'Vietnam Introduces Maritime Law', VietNamNetBridge, 17 July 2012, http://english.vietnamnet.vn/fms/government/24535/vietnam-introduces-maritime-law.html. For Chinese reactions see 'China Opposes Vietnamese Maritime Law over Sovereignty Claims', Xinhua, 21 June 2012, http://news.xinhuanet.com/english/china/2012-06/21/c_131668632.htm.

[24] Fravel, 'Maritime Security in the South China Sea and the Competition over Maritime Rights', p. 43.

[25] 'Philippines "to take South China Sea Row to Court"', *BBC News*, 22 January 2013.

[26] See, for example: UNCLOS Part XV for a description of dispute settlement procedures; UNCLOS Part XI, Section V for ITLOS' role on seabed disputes; the ITLOS website (www.itlos.org) for a description of the chambers maintained by the tribunal; and the ICJ's website (www.icj-cij.org) for an outline of cases that can be brought to the court.

[27] William Choong, 'Manila Deals a Clever Hand with Desire for Arbitration', *Straits Times*, 30 January 2013.

[28] Daniel Ten Kate, 'Russia to Help Vietnam Produce Anti-ship Missiles, RIA says', *Bloomberg News*, 16 February 2012. http://www.bloomberg.com/news/2012-02-16/russia-to-help-vietnam-produce-anti-ship-missiles-ria-says-1-.html.

[29] Other US vessels have been repaired in other shipyards: the first vessel was repaired in 2009 in Saigon. Thayer, 'Vietnam Looking to Play Pivotal Role with both China and US', *Global Times*, 25 July 2012, http://www.globaltimes.cn/content/723033.shtml.

30  Kagan, 'The Vietnam Solution'.

31  For Beijing's perspective, see, for example, the comments by Zhou Shouwei, former deputy general manager of CNOOC Group in: 'China Researcher: China hasn't yet Exploited "Mid-Southern" South China Sea', Dow Jones Newswires, 2 July 2012.

32  'Operations in the South China Sea', Oilfield Technology, June 2011, http://www.slb.com/~/media/Files/coiled_tubing/industry_articles/201108_ct_operations_south_china_sea.pdf.

33  International Crisis Group, 'Stirring up the South China Sea II: Regional Responses', June 2012, p. 42.

34  'China, Brunei Pledge Further Cooperation', Xinhua, 30 January 2013, http://english.peopledaily.com.cn/90883/8115346.html.

35  See for example comments by Indonesian Foreign Minister Marty Natalegawa that the status quo in the South China Sea is 'not an option'. Daniel Ten Kate and Karl Lester M. Yap, 'Risk of Conflict in South China Sea is Set to Prompt ASEAN Pact with China', Bloomberg, 21 July 2011, http://www.bloomberg.com/news/2011-07-20/china-asean-to-agree-on-incomplete-s-china-sea-rules.html.

36  Sabam Siagian, 'The Un-ASEAN Way of Treating Unresolved Issues', Jakarta Post, 16 July 2012, http://www.thejakartapost.com/news/2012/07/16/the-un-asean-way-treating-unresolved-issues.html.

37  Thayer, 'Behind the Scenes of ASEAN's Breakdown', Asia Times, 27 July 2012.

38  In 1995, whilst again failing to clarify China's precise claims, a PRC spokesman did note that China had no dispute with Indonesia.

39  'Govt to Ramp Up Troops in Natuna', Antara [Indonesian National News Agency], 25 May 2012, http://www.accessmylibrary.com/article-1G1-290808210/govt-ramp-up-troops.html.

40  Ristian Atriandi Supriyanto, 'Indonesia's South China Sea Dilemma: Between Neutrality and Self-Interest', RSIS Commentary 126, 2012.

41  'Petronas in Joint Vietnam Venture', The Star [Malaysia], 9 January 2002.

42  See, for example: 'TNI Expects Stronger Navy Fleet by 2024', Jakarta Post, 30 August 2012, http://www.thejakartapost.com/news/2012/08/30/tni-expects-stronger-navy-fleet-2024.html.

43  Janeman Latul and Neil Chatterjee, 'Infrastructure as the Missing BRIC in Indonesia's Wall', Reuters, 19 January 2012, http://uk.reuters.com/article/2012/01/19/idUKL3E8CJ68F20120119.

44  Statement by Singapore Foreign Ministry 2011, cited in: 'Singapore urges China to Clarify South China Sea Claim', BBC News, 20 June 2011, http://www.bbc.co.uk/news/world-asia-pacific-13838462.

45  Philip Bowring, 'Singapore Quiets the South China Sea', Asia Sentinel, 29 June 2011.

46  For example Su Hao, from China Foreign Affairs University, commented to China Daily, that 'Sino-Thai cooperation is expected to serve as an example for China's ties with other ASEAN nations'. Zhou Wa, 'China's ASEAN Role Wins Praise', China Daily, 17 April 2012, http://www.chinadaily.

com.cn/china/2012-04/17/
content_15063180.htm.

47 *Ibid.*

48 The Philippine Foreign Secretary
reportedly offered to soften
mention of recent clashes with
simply a passing reference to 'the
affected shoal', yet even this was
dismissed with limited attempt to
find common ground reportedly
made.

49 Von Sokheng and Shane Worrell,
'Hu Pledges Millions in Aid', *Phnom
Penh Post*, 2 April 2012.

50 'China Gives Cambodia Aid
and Thanks for ASEAN Help',
Reuters, 4 September 2012,
http://www.reuters.com/
article/2012/09/04/us-cambodia-
china-idUSBRE88306I20120904.

51 Prak Chan Thul, 'Hu Wants
Cambodia Help on China Sea
Dispute, Pledges Aid', Reuters, 31
March 2012.

52 *Ibid.*

53 'Chinese Official Lauds Cambodian
Support for Beijing's Core Interests',
Xinhua, 3 December 2012.

54 Kavi Chongkittavorn, 'Thailand
Walks a Tightrope on the South
China Sea', *The Nation*, 7 May 2012,
http://www.nationmultimedia.
com/opinion/Thailand-walks-
a-tightrope-on-South-China-
Sea-30181423.html.

55 Jeremy Grant, Ben Bland and
Gwen Robinson, 'South China Sea
Issue Divides Asean', *Financial
Times*, 16 July 2012, http://
www.ft.com/cms/s/0/3d45667c-
cf29-11e1-bfd9-00144feabdco.
html#axzz2JTyEEgny.

56 Interview with an adviser to the
King of Cambodia, Shangri-La
Dialogue, 2 June 2012.

57 For further details see International
Crisis Group, 'Stirring up the South
China Sea II: Regional Responses',
Asia Report no. 229, 24 July 2012, p.
16.

58 Jens Kastner, 'Taiwan Circling
South China Sea Bait', *Asia Times*,
13 June 2012.

59 See, for example, comments made
by former Deputy Chief of the
General Staff Admiral Fei Hung-po.
Quoted in: Chan, 'Sea Row Chance
to Foster New Ties', *SCMP*, 3 June
2012.

60 See, for example, the 2012
announcement of a special airborne
unit able to reach Taiping Island
with the help of C-130 aircraft
within four hours. 'Taiwan Sets up
Airborne Unit for Spratlys', Agence
France-Presse, 2 May 2012.

61 In lieu of any agreement, the
Philippines reportedly led the way
in demanding a record be made
of the fact that the South China
Sea had been discussed whereas
Cambodia argued that such mention
compromised ASEAN neutrality.
Simon Tay, 'ASEAN, Neutral or
Neutered?', *Today Online*, 17 July
2012.

62 'Severe Dent on ASEAN Credibility',
*Singapore Straits Times*, 14 July 2012;
Jeremy Grant, Ben Bland and Gwen
Robinson, 'South China Sea Issue
Divides Asean'.

63 Jason Szep and James Pomfret,
'Tensions Flare over South China
Sea at ASEAN Summit', Reuters, 19
November 2012.

64 Jon Grevatt, 'Thailand Agrees to
German Submarine Procurement',
*Jane's Defence Weekly*, 23 March 2011.

65 Jaime Laude, 'Philippine Navy
needs P500B to Upgrade War

Capability', *Philippine Star*, 24 May 2012, http://www.philstar.com/breaking-news/809955/philippine-navy-needs-p500b-upgrade-war-capability.

66 Taiwan has been studying the feasibility of such an indigenous programme for several years. See: Wendell Minnick, 'Taiwan to Build Own Subs', *Defense News*, 13 April 2009.

67 George Amurao, 'Philippines Builds Anti-China Muscle', *Asia Times*, 2 March 2012, http://www.atimes.com/atimes/Southeast_Asia/NC02Ae01.html.

68 Tim Huxley, *Defending the Lion City: The Armed Forces of Singapore* (St Leonards, NSW: Allen & Unwin 2000), pp. 33–4.

69 Quoted in: Yoichi Kato, 'South China Sea Disputes: Harbinger of Regional Strategic Shift?', p. 4.

70 Frances Mangosing, 'Philippines to Receive 10 New Patrol Ships from Japan', *Philippine Daily Inquirer*, 18 May 2012.

71 Raisa Robles, 'Japan Offers Philippines 10 Ships to Patrol South China Sea', *South China Morning Post*, 11 January 2013.

72 'Japan PM Shinzo Abe Begins Southeast Asia Push in Vietnam', *BBC News*, 16 January 2013.

73 Mangosing, 'Philippines to Buy 12 South Korean Fighter Jets', *Inquirer.net*, 31 January 2013, http://newsinfo.inquirer.net/350421/philippines-to-buy-12-south-korean-fighter-jets.

74 'China Pushes India–ASEAN Towards Strategic Partnership', *iSikkim*, 16 February 2012, http://isikkim.com/2012-02-china-pushes-india-asean-towards-

strategic-partnership-16-06/; 'After Kailakunda, Singapore to Train at Indian Army Firing Ranges', *Indian Express*, 12 August 2008, http://www.indianexpress.com/news/after-kalaikunda-singapore-to-train-at-indian-army-firing-ranges/348181.

75 Ananth Krishnan, 'South China Sea Projects 'Risky for India'', *The Hindu*, 5 April 2012, http://www.thehindu.com/news/international/article3281437.ece.

76 Krishnan, 'In South China Sea, a Surprise Chinese Escort for Indian Ships', *The Hindu*, 14 June 2012, http://www.thehindu.com/news/national/article3524965.ece?homepage=true.

77 Edna Curran, 'Australia has Role in China Sea Dispute', *Wall Street Journal*, 13 September 2012, http://online.wsj.com/article/SB10000872396390444709004577650124046496702.html.

78 'Vietnam Allows Russia to Set Up Ship Maintenance Base at Port in Cam Ranh Bay', CNTV, 30 July 2012, http://english.cntv.cn/program/newshour/20120730/110324.shtml; 'Russia Seeks to Set Up Naval Bases Abroad', Associated Press, 27 July 2012.

79 For full text of 2012 EU East Asia Policy Guidelines, see: http://eeas.europa.eu/asia/docs/guidelines_eu_foreign_sec_pol_east_asia_en.pdf.

80 See, for example: 'UK to Deepen Engagement with ASEAN', Xinhua, 27 June 2012.

81 For more on the RCEP and the differences with the TPP, see: Murray Hiebert and Liam Hanlon 'ASEAN and Partners Launch

Regional Comprehensive Economic Partnership', CSIS, 7 December 2012, http://csis.org/publication/ asean-and-partners-launch-regional-comprehensive-economic-partnership.

# CHAPTER FOUR

# The US in the South China Sea

Since at least the end of the twentieth century, it has been increasingly evident that the evolution of US–China relations will prove a major determinant in the history of the twenty-first. Whilst China has been making considerable diplomatic and economic inroads in Asia, so the US has been reminding the same continent of its Pacific power, working to increase not only its diplomatic and economic investments in the region, but also its strategic and military ones. Within Southeast Asia, the US has treaty alliances with the Philippines and Thailand, as well as important security partnerships with other countries including Singapore and Indonesia.

Within this context, the rise of the South China Sea as a global as well as a regional security concern should come as no surprise. As this book has argued, tensions surrounding the South China Sea are not based exclusively on claimant inter-pretations of history and demands of sovereignty, or contested access to hydrocarbons and fisheries; they also involve concerns of grand strategy. As issues such as the impact of China's naval modernisation, or the future of the US forward-deployed pres-ence in the region and the balance of power in Asia are debated, so the South China Sea becomes a natural focal point for attention. Tensions here both feed into and reflect the evolution of Asia-Pacific relations, recasting the disputes, as well as ASEAN member states' abilities to manage them, into a broader strategic framework. And it is this backdrop that makes the disputes both more volatile and more dangerous with regard to the potential ramifications that could flow from any misjudgement.

In these circumstances, the sea understandably attracts the attention – including through the conduct of intelligence-gathering activities – of the US as the pre-eminent naval power, as well as of other regional powers. So it is that, even if other tensions, including concerns over the safeguarding of unimpeded commerce, could be satisfactorily resolved, there would still remain some intractability to the broader strategic dynamic of evident mistrust. Meanwhile, questions over the rights of navies to undertake exercises and gather intelligence within the EEZ of another state – a debate that is presently focused on the South China Sea – have obvious global ramifications. In the word of US Naval War College Professor Peter Dutton, 'China's challenge to existing maritime norms is creating hair-line fractures in a global order'.[1]

It is in the semi-enclosed South China Sea, where the region's restricted geography benefits littoral states and where the US does not have any permanent bases, that China's naval modernisation is most likely to challenge US naval hegemony, at least at a localised level. It is no surprise then, that an increase in the attention paid to Asia was on the US foreign-policy agenda well before the inauguration of America's 'first Pacific President'.[2] Since 2000, Asia has been the largest source of US imports and second-largest market for exports after the North American region.[3] Fast-growing economies and populations have further highlighted the increasing importance of Asian markets for the US economy. Under the G.W. Bush administration, the development of existing relationships with key regional allies had been prioritised and a move towards a lighter, more flexible military presence begun. The administration of President Barack Obama, in turn, sharpened and upgraded this thinking in the deliberate promotion of the US as an Asia-Pacific power.[4]

## Obama's Asia pivot

In late 2011, the Obama administration announced its Asia 'pivot' which was quickly relabelled a 'rebalance' in many quarters concerned about insinuations of a schizophrenic superpower. This outlined American intentions to intensify focus on the Asia-Pacific and was aimed, in part, at shaping the development of regional norms. The idea was to bolster the US presence in the region and reduce uncertainty there regarding its commitments, whilst also warning China away from any temptation, resulting from its growing capabilities, to employ more heavy-handed tactics in pursuit of its national interests. Indeed, whilst the US reminded those who would listen that the pivot was not all about China, the Joint Chiefs of Staff's *2011 National Military Strategy* was already clear in its intention to pay more attention to the challenges posed by China's development. In order to help deal with the insecurities these developments are creating, a US presence in the region is now seen from Washington's perspective at least as 'the essential ingredient for stability'.[5]

Within this reiterated US commitment, the South China Sea has assumed an important tangible and symbolic role. Speaking in 2011, National Security Advisor Tom Donilon referred to the sea's significance as he explained the pivot in terms of US national interests in ensuring that 'commerce and freedom of navigation are not impeded ... and that disagreements are resolved peacefully without threats or coercion'.[6] More broadly, US approaches to this sea are shaping regional perceptions of its commitments to Asia, as well as Chinese perceptions as to the extent of US 'external' interference.

There are, therefore, some risks associated with the pivot. Much has been made of the initiative in public-relations terms, in particular in Southeast Asia, to the extent that any apparent failure to follow through would have considerable consequences for US credibility in the region. Moreover, despite US efforts to frame its increased engagement as being focused on something more than the management of China's rise, there is little doubt that it has fuelled Chinese suspicions of US intentions, further adding to the levels of mistrust between these two important partners.

## Military modernisation and the evolution of US partnerships in the region

As has been explored in the previous chapter, the events of 11 September 2001 had already provided considerable impetus for the US to enhance its military cooperation with the countries of Southeast Asia through the search to deny breeding grounds for future terrorists or facilities agents. Military cooperation with the Philippines, Thailand and Singapore, amongst others, was duly reinforced. In this regard, the annual *Balikatan* exercises are perhaps the most explicit example of an increasing US military presence and engagement with an ally in order to tackle the perceived threat from transnational terrorist organisations – in this case Jemaah Islamiyah and the Abu Sayyaf group. Further examples of this increased US engagement in the region include the multilateral *Rim of the Pacific* exercise (RIMPAC), the largest international maritime exercise, and the annual *Cobra Gold* exercises held in Thailand, which are now regarded as the US's primary multilateral military ground exercise in the region.[7] By 2012, 20 nations were participating in these exercises, including seven – the US, Thailand, Indonesia, Japan, Malaysia, Singapore and South Korea – as contributing forces.

In a similar vein, in 2005, US Pacific Command launched Cooperation Afloat Readiness and Training (CARAT) with its series of mainly bilateral, annual exercises focused on counter-piracy and aimed at bolstering naval interoperability between the US and partner nations, as well as increasing the capabilities of those partner nations, which now include all ASEAN member states with the exception of Laos, Myanmar and Vietnam.[8] Meanwhile, the first US unified maritime strategy – presented in 2007 and entitled 'A cooperative strategy for the 21st century' – explains the defence of the freedom of navigation and commerce as a 'core capability' of US naval forces, committing the US to being able to 'impose local sea control wherever necessary, ideally with our friends and allies, but by ourselves if we must'.[9]

As the terrorist threat receded, and attention returned, later in the decade, towards more traditional issues of geopolitics, these initiatives were tweaked towards building up US capabilities more broadly, as well as those of their partners and allies in the region. In particular, as the realities of the US fiscal situation became clear, Washington began to move away from its traditional 'hub-and-spokes' model of alliance operations, towards the construction of a more diffuse and distributed network. It would work with partners to build up their security capabilities, and would support their efforts to partner with each other as well as with the US. This has led to the nascent development of a 'spokes-to-spokes' system, whereby US allies who previously relied largely on bilateral American security guarantees are now building stronger military–military relations between themselves. Although some of these developments are occurring under the guidance of the US, through multilateral mechanisms (such as the 2007 iteration of the US–India *Malabar* exercises, which also involved assets from Japan, Singapore and Australia), bilateral exchanges are also slowly proliferating – the Japanese–Australian *Nichi Gou Trident* exercises held in June 2012 are a good example of this. These exchanges will not be restricted only to the most significant US allies in the region. In his speech to the Shangri-La Dialogue in 2012, then US Defense Secretary Leon Panetta specifically cited the US intention to enhance partnerships with Indonesia, Malaysia, India, Vietnam and New Zealand.

Meanwhile, non-deployed US engagement has stretched beyond combat exercises with traditional allies and begun to include states that were formerly antagonistic towards American influence in the region. In particular, the US has been slowly and carefully developing a defence dialogue with Vietnam, perhaps the most vocal Southeast Asian protagonist in the South China Sea. This comes as part of a relationship that remains particularly complex and sensitive, especially given ongoing ideological differences between the two governments and a history that means that more than 20% of the country continues to be affected by unexploded US ordnance.[10] Nevertheless, whilst good relations with China continue to be important for Vietnam, in particular in economic terms, there appears to be a mutual interest between the US and Vietnam in balancing these closer links with the cautious upgrading of their own bilateral ties. In 2010, a US–Vietnam annual defence policy dialogue was launched, having been first initiated in 2004 and then elevated to the level of a political, security and defence dialogue in 2008.[11] A Memorandum of Understanding resulted from the second of these policy dialogues in 2011. Meanwhile, the US Navy has been making port calls to Vietnam annually since 2003, when the USS *Vandergrift* docked in Ho

Chi Minh City. In recent years, such visits have become both more frequent and been upgraded, including, for example, the first visit of a US aircraft carrier to Vietnamese waters in 2010.

Engagement and exercises are just one way in which the US has set about building stronger relationships in the region. Alongside knowledge and training, it has also been providing hardware in its quest to boost regional security capabilities. This is perhaps most apparent in the support the US has been providing to its oldest treaty ally in Asia, the Philippines, aimed at boosting the still severely limited military capabilities of the country's navy. Although the *Hamilton*-class cutters the US has gifted to date boast only minimal combat capabilities (equipped with only a 76mm gun and .50 calibre machine guns), the first vessel donated is now the flagship of the Philippine navy. The vessels are also likely to be upgraded in the future with anti-ship missiles. Meanwhile, in 2012, the US allocated US$30m in military financing for the Philippines – a noticeable improvement on the US$11.9m budgeted the previous year.[12]

Of course, the US has also been seeking a more direct, deployed presence in the region, albeit of a modest, distributed and flexible nature. Access rather than bases has become the mantra. The November 2011 announcement that US marines would be rotated on a six-monthly basis through Darwin, Australia, reaching a force of 2,500 by 2017, and that more access would also be given to US naval and air vessels, was a clear reflection of this strategy. Similar thinking lay behind the announcement earlier in the year of the stationing in Singapore of two US forward-deployed Littoral Combat Ships – vessels designed to operate in the littoral waters near a coastline. This was then increased to four in 2012, with the first vessels being deployed in 2013.

The US may yet coax other countries in the region into similar models of cooperation. Two decades after evicting

US forces from what was their largest naval base in Asia, the Philippines is, for example, considering once again inviting a more substantial US military presence onto its territory.[13] China's military advancements are bringing a convergence in strategic interests, resulting in the expansion of cooperation beyond the fight against transnational, non-state armed groups with Islamist ideals to include the improvement of maritime defences. This is important for the Philippines in terms of sovereignty disputes in the South China Sea, and for the US from the broader perspective of protecting US freedom of maritime action in the face of Chinese naval advancements. Domestic political sensitivities can be catered to by an emphasis on the transient and flexible nature of any arrangement, whilst rotational policies can afford both a near-continuous presence and the necessary veneer of temporariness. Certainly concerns over their sovereignty claims in the South China Sea help keep Southeast Asian nations receptive to such compromises, cognisant as they are to the security advantages that come from an ongoing US presence in the region, as a balance to growing Chinese military might. As the Philippine Foreign Affairs Secretary Albert del Rosario commented in 2012, in a call for more joint-training exercises akin to *Balikatan* and on a bigger scale, 'we would like the Americans to come more often'.[14]

Yet the reality is that, for the moment, these US deployments remain relatively humble, and are only one part of the entire US 'pivot' strategy for Asia. In fact, the pivot is as much as rebalance *within* the region as a rebalance *towards* the region. Alongside the new deployments to Singapore and Australia, plus the possibility of an increased rotation of forces through the Philippines, in April 2012 the US also agreed a revised agreement to relocate approximately 9,000 marines from Okinawa in Japan to Guam, Hawaii and Australia. The decision reflects new US strategies in the region, encapsulated in the Joint Operational Access Concept (JOAC), which was released within two weeks of Obama and Panetta's January 2012 announcement of the overall pivot strategy. The JOAC, and the unpublished and classified AirSea Battle Concept (ASBC) which nests within JOAC,[15] are part of a military strategy that favours a dispersal of forces in order to counter A2AD capabilities of a rival.[16] For the US, which has, since the end of the Cold War, enjoyed unchallenged access to the global maritime domain including the South China Sea, the JOAC and ASBC are an attempt to continue to protect this privilege. They encourage closer coordination between different services, as well as the use of dispersed forces in several bases to operate on 'multiple, independent lines of operations', with the intention of bringing these forces to 'manoeuvre directly against key operational objectives from strategic distance'.[17]

The US aims to benefit from the dispersal of its forces through East Asia in terms of both its relations with China as well as with the broader region. The pragmatic removal of troops out of the range of some Chinese missiles has the ancillary benefit of suggesting to Beijing that this is a defensive rather than aggressive change to the status quo. Meanwhile, the broader distribution of troops allows for stronger relationships to be built with a wider number of allies, thus creating a more robust defensive posture, to counter China's asymmetric capabilities.[18]

However, it is questionable whether Beijing has viewed the US pivot as entirely defensive. It is also worth noting that the pivot has had some unexpected effects that demonstrate the latent mistrust regarding its presence in the region. For example, Thailand's failure in 2012 to grant permission to NASA to use U-Tapao naval air base for a project entitled 'Southeast Asia Composition, Cloud, Climate Coupling Regional Study' was largely owing to domestic criticism and concerns over a possible military application for the project. Nonetheless, there has been a clear attempt to reposition the US towards and within East Asia, so as to encourage greater interactions with and among allies, and help to build capacity in weaker states. In particular, the repositioning US forces themselves aims to reassure allies and keep a check on China.

## Building stronger political and economic partnerships

Whilst defence remains the centrepiece of a reworked programme to promote the US presence in the region, it comes packaged with an understanding that this commitment has to be more broadly conceived. In particular, it should be grounded in the institutionalisation of a stronger US political and economic presence in the region. Diplomatically, this involves developing a regular dialogue of strategic discussions about the region's future, thereby helping to shore up the logic for a strong US presence in the region. This includes the simple task of 'showing up' – a critique long held by Southeast Asian nations against the Bush administration, with George W. Bush opting to miss, amongst other occasions, the 2007 US–ASEAN summit which celebrated 30 years of US–ASEAN relations. Meanwhile, Bush's Secretary of State Condoleezza Rice missed two of her last three meetings of the ASEAN Regional Forum, with US representation also notably absent from commercial events, such as the December 2005 ASEAN Business and Investment meeting.[19] At this time, the South China Sea remained limited to a regional rather than a global concern, and a territorial rather than a strategic one.

In contrast, in 2009 and 2010, then Secretary of State Hillary Clinton visited the Asia-Pacific on at least eight separate occasions, including her first official visit overseas. Instead of making the traditional first trip to Europe, she toured Japan, Indonesia, South Korea and China. Furthermore, Obama's first overseas visit after winning re-election in November 2012 was to Thailand, Myanmar and Cambodia, making him the first serving US president to visit the latter two countries.[20] During Clinton's time in office, her travels included addressing a meeting of the ASEAN Regional Forum in July 2010, at which she set out the US 'national interest' in open access to the South China Sea and specifically cited US commitments to freedom of navigation, unimpeded commerce, the upholding of international law, and the need for peaceful resolution. Whilst China was quick to accuse the US of a cynical exploitation of regional tensions, a number of smaller and medium-sized powers in the region were privately appreciative of the signal that Clinton sent. Meanwhile, Obama has regularly participated in meetings between the US and ASEAN, including at a first US–ASEAN leaders meeting in Singapore in 2009. (The joint statement of the second US–ASEAN leaders meeting in 2010 duly raised the issue of maritime security, freedom of navigation, and respect for international law, including UNCLOS.[21]) In July 2009, the US signed the Treaty of Amity and Cooperation, thereby paving the way for it to participate in the EAS from 2011. There, it was able to support concerned Southeast Asian partners in ensuring that discussions on the South China Sea made it on to the agenda, whilst again making clear its position on key issues of maritime security, including freedom of navigation and over-flight in the South China Sea.[22]

For those who remain particularly sceptical of ASEAN's ability to manage the issues surrounding the South China Sea, US membership of the East Asia Summit should potentially prove of special significance. This is particularly the case since the US appears to have chosen to use its membership to push a forum which has traditionally focused more on economic cooperation towards one where political and security issues are also discussed.

In another sign of the Obama administration's increased commitment to regional multilateralism, in 2010 the US became the first non-ASEAN country to establish a dedicated mission to ASEAN, with a permanent ambassador in place from 2011. The links developed here have been important in facilitating US work with ASEAN to place the South China Sea, against Chinese wishes, onto the agendas of regional meetings, and to push for a new Code of Conduct. For example, and as identified by a discontented China, the US was active in pushing onto the agenda of the July 2010 ASEAN Regional Forum the tabling of concerns by 12 countries over recent developments in the South China Sea. Likewise, whilst recognising the process has to at least appear ASEAN-owned, once the guidelines of July 2011 seemed to re-commit China to the pursuit of a code, the US worked hard behind the scenes with ASEAN to support continued momentum on this issue. Publicly, Panetta reminded those involved that this opportunity should not be wasted by the signing of just any code. It was important that it was 'binding' and would 'create a rules-based framework for regulating the conduct of parties'.[23] Privately, US officials even offered their own draft version for ASEAN consideration – to the considerable ire of China.[24]

Given the broad nature of US objectives and its interests in shaping debates on the development of regional norms and values, such outreach has, of course, not simply been confined to the littoral states of Southeast Asia most prominent in the South China Sea disputes. Considerable work is also being done elsewhere. For example, in 2009, the US launched a new US–Lower Mekong Initiative aimed at developing cooperation between the US, Cambodia, Thailand, Laos and Vietnam on issues ranging from environmental protection to education, infrastructure and healthcare. In July 2012, on her way to a meeting with ASEAN counterparts, Hillary Clinton became the first US secretary of state to visit Laos in 57 years.

The development of a coherent trade policy to the region has perhaps been the weakest part of this reinvigorated political and economic engagement with Southeast Asia. Since the turn of the century, the US has been making some efforts bilaterally to promote trading relations with individual Southeast Asian nations, in part for obvious economic reasons, but also in part driven by consideration of the broader strategic context. It does have, for example, a Free Trade Agreement with Singapore, dating back to 2003, and a Trade and Investment Framework Agreement was concluded between the US and ASEAN in 2006. However, similar initiatives with Malaysia and Thailand proved unsuccessful. With ASEAN already having agreed a free-trade area with China, and with discussions underway with other Asian powers such as South Korea, the US already has some catching up to do.

Nonetheless, the US remains a crucial commercial partner in the region, especially with regard to investment. In the case of Cambodia, for example, many economic indices may highlight its close interactions with China, but around half of all of the country's exports still go to the US, which remains its largest market for clothing and footwear products.[25] Likewise it is the US, rather than China, that serves as Vietnam's largest export market. More generally, in 2011, the Asia-Pacific accounted for over 60% of total goods exported by the US and nearly three-quarters of all agricultural exports.[26] Collectively the ASEAN countries are the fourth-largest trading partner of the US, with trade totalling US$178bn in 2010.[27]

The announcement by the Obama administration in 2009 that the US would join negotiations for a Trans-Pacific Partnership (TPP) is an ambitious step forward. At the time of writing, 11 Pacific economies – notably not including China

– are involved in talks to conclude a far-reaching trade agreement amongst partner countries. Agreement here is also seen as a key pathway to broader Asia-Pacific regional economic integration. Any realisation of this aim, but potentially even the very process of negotiation towards it, serves to reinforce the central US role in the Asia-Pacific, not simply in terms of presence but also in terms of values. TPP proposals under discussion include provisions to help ensure that state-owned enterprises have to compete on a level playing field with private enterprise, to tackle trade and investment barriers faced by SMEs, and to address problems of 'indigenous innovation' so often raised in relation to China. However, even assuming a successful conclusion to negotiations, the prospect is not without significant practical constraints from a US perspective – not least concerns over its ability to actually join any partnership given its present difficulties in passing trade deals through Congress, as evidenced by the severely delayed adoption of the US–South Korean FTA in 2011.[28]

## Constraining factors on US engagement

Money is perhaps the most obvious potential limitation on US ambitions to defend its naval pre-eminence, including in the South China Sea, and prove a key influence in the ongoing development of the Asia-Pacific. For many, including America's partners in Southeast Asia, it remains far from clear that the US can fulfil its commitment to decrease substantially its defence budgets by at least US$489bn between 2012 and 2022, whilst simultaneously strengthening its presence in the Asia-Pacific. Repeated diplomatic dismissals of fears to the contrary do little to reassure. Despite pledges that reductions in defence spending will not come at the expense of the Asia-Pacific, Panetta was still forced to admit to journalists at a meeting of ASEAN defence ministers in 2011, 'There's no question that

... concerns have been expressed.'[29] Reassurance will come only through sustained experience of engagement, including through the regular conduct of sea patrols and joint exercises.

Indeed, when Panetta finally put more flesh onto the military aspect of Obama's Asia pivot, the scarce resources available were evident for all to see. This big new policy initiative appeared, in reality, to contain little substantively new. It stipulated that 60% of the US's air and naval forces would from now on be concentrated in the Pacific, and this would 'include six aircraft carriers in this region, a majority of our cruisers, destroyers, Littoral Combat Ships, and submarines'.[30] But as the IISS's Tim Huxley noted in a lively debate that followed on the credibility of this US commitment, 'the US had six aircraft carriers in the Pacific at least as long ago as 2007, and most US Navy submarines (38 out of 67) and both Littoral Combat Ships (LCS) are also already in this region. One has to ask if moving a few extra USN destroyers and frigates, and deploying a few LCS to Singapore, is really going to make much difference to the regional military balance during the rest of this decade.'[31]

Ideology also remains a powerful variable in the quest for influence in the region. Throughout much of the first decade of the twenty-first century, whilst Southeast Asian states and the US could find common ground over concerns about the rise of radical Islam, there were domestic political limitations to any cohabitation, at least in Southeast Asia's three Muslim majority states. More generally, the diverse nature of Southeast Asian governments ensures that the precise impact of the US commitment to concepts of democracy, individual human rights and enlightened intervention remains mixed. However, there can be no doubt that for many in the region the US can be a problematic partner in its insistence on giving voice to its values. By contrast, China can appear the more low-maintenance partner. Vietnam, Laos and Cambodia for example, still have more in common with China's thinking on the inviolability of domestic politics and the sanctity of 'non-interference' than they do with the US outlook on these issues. As noted in the previous chapter, this same ideational scale also acts as an important brake on ASEAN's own development. There is then, perhaps, some irony in the fact that some of ASEAN's perceived ineffectiveness in particular regard to the South China Sea has actually encouraged claimant countries such as the Philippines and even Vietnam to look beyond ASEAN for support, and actively seek US engagement.

For some, Washington's own failure to ratify UNCLOS also serves unnecessarily to stymie its influence in the South China Sea disputes. More specifically, it constrains the US voice in the unfolding debate on naval rights of passage within an EEZ, as Chinese interpretations are made more apparent and, in some countries such as Malaysia and India, to some extent supported in the face of espoused US national interests and positions.[32] Obama's failure in 2012 to secure the two-thirds majority necessary in the US Senate that would allow for ratification, despite vocal support from his administration and many in the US military, was widely seen as seriously problematic by supporters of UNCLOS. As Panetta argued at the time, 'We potentially undercut our credibility in a number of Asia-focused multilateral venues – just as we're pushing for a rules-based order in the region and the peaceful resolution of maritime and territorial disputes in the South China Sea … How can we argue that other nations must abide by international rules, when we haven't officially accepted those rules?'[33]

The treaty, which came into force in 1994 and which effectively establishes the rights and responsibilities of states with regard to the use of the world's seas, has been signed by the European Union and more than 160 countries, but not the US. However, as popular as this cause has become in the mainstream commentariat in the US and overseas, and as much as the US could theoretically gain greater moral standing and a stronger legal position from ratification, there are reasons for caution. The reality is that whilst the US failure to ratify might be a convenient political stick with which those interested in doing so anyway can castigate the country for double standards, ratification would, in fact, add only limited credibility, whilst possibly also opening up the US to further diplomatic and legal wrangling in search of a tighter definition for an already contentious law. Maritime disputes in the South China Sea are at their heart about power politics; international law needs to remain the key frame of reference, but a sole focus on this framework becomes problematic when interpretations of that law are unclear and are still being contested. Meanwhile, China is likely to continue conducting military activity within the claimed EEZs of others, whilst attempting to deny the US similar rights by citation of UNCLOS.

Another further constraint on US engagement is the limit on alliance-building in Southeast Asia demanded by US national interests beyond the South China Sea. As Germany and the UK manoeuvred before the First World War to construct alliances designed to deter conflict, the dominoes of commitments engendered ended up actually helping to fan the flames of war.[34] The danger for the US is that it ends up creating expectations it may not want to meet, taking on actual or perceived commitments that force it towards a crossroads it might otherwise seek to avoid: the decision to stand by an ally or partner on principle and risk an escalation on a matter not of fundamental national interest, or to be seen to have their bluff called, thereby bringing into question the core credibility of US commitments in the region. This is particularly the case with regard to the Philippines, with whom the US has a Mutual Defence Agreement, certainly applicable to the Western Pacific but questionably applicable to the South China Sea. As the Philippines sent its US-donated cutter to arrest Chinese fishermen off Scarborough Reef in April 2012, the US had a delicate balance to strike in the support it proffered. A '2+2' meeting in May between the foreign and defence ministers of the two countries stressed Washington's strategic ambiguity on the issue: while reaffirming the 1951 San Francisco Treaty, US diplomats also highlighted their country's neutrality on the South China Sea sovereignty disputes. Whilst Secretary of State Clinton therefore explicitly stated that the US would protect freedom of navigation in the South China Sea, she notably neglected to mention whether the defence treaty extended to disputed areas of the sea. The message sent was clear in its equivocality and is similar to the US position on Taiwan: while the US will help the Philippines develop its military and will protect undisputed Philippine territory, it cannot afford to provide a carte blanche for defending disputed areas claimed by the Philippines.

## Considering China

The US has gone some way towards attempting to counter Chinese concerns both with regard to the agenda underlying its Asia pivot, in general, and its interests in the South China Sea, in particular. Although Chinese diplomatic statements have generally been relatively restrained in their response to the pivot, military commentary, including in some of the Chinese press, has often been more critical, for example with accusations that the US continues to suffer from a 'Cold War mentality'.[35] Privately, many officials are concerned by what they see as both an unwarranted and unwelcome attempt to undermine Chinese influence in the region. Statements of US support for a greater (rules-based) role in the region are therefore important. As Obama told then Chinese Vice President Xi Jinping during a White House meeting in early 2012, in order for the US to strengthen its relationships in the region and be a 'strong and effective partner with the Asia Pacific ... it is absolutely vital that we have a strong relationship with China'.[36]

Even when any belief in the achievability of a closer collaborative relationship, held at the outset of the first Obama administration, had fallen away, senior officials in his administration made clear efforts to develop a cooperative partnership with China, both through the regularity of their trips and the nature of the briefs they carried. For example, towards the end of his tenure as secretary of defense, Robert Gates was noticeable in his determination to build a closer and more stable dialogue between the two militaries, even as Chinese paramilitaries were moving aggressively against Vietnamese and Philippine survey ships in the South China Sea.[37]

However, the reality is that the military–military relationship between the US and China remains heavy on protocol and light on content, and has long lagged behind the development of broader political and economic relations. It has also been subject to repeated periods of friction, whether over US concerns following the Tiananmen Square killings of 1989, or, more recently, the occasional temporary suspensions of certain or all forms of engagement by China as a punitive tool to signal dissatisfaction with the US in another policy area. For example, China cut off military–military relations in January 2010 in retaliation for Washington's announcement that it would fulfil an arms order with Taiwan, with relations only revived in December 2010 in the form of the US–China Defense Consultative Talks (DCT).

The DCT, which was first held in December 1997, is the oldest of a number of military–military forums in which the two countries are engaged, closely followed by the Military Maritime Consultative Agreement (MMCA), which is an annual consultative process that aims to discuss 'measures to promote safe practices and establish mutual trust' at sea. In December 2006, annual Defense Policy Coordination Talks were also established, with a hotline agreed at the second session. Finally, the Strategic Security Dialogue, which was created in May 2011, is focused on crisis management and the provision of a mechanism for civilian and military leaders to discuss issues of mutual importance. Meanwhile, high-level bilateral talks and reciprocal visits continue to offer important confidence-building measures, with the US Navy announcing in 2012 that the PLAN would be invited to attend RIMPAC in 2014.

The steady growth in military–military engagements indicates a desire on both sides to avoid costly misunderstandings as their forces increasingly come into contact with each other in the air and at sea. Yet the mechanisms that have been created thus far are purely consultative and have not introduced rules-based regimes to US–Chinese interactions. This means that considerable scope for misinterpretation remains and that there is little confining the two sides to predictable patterns of behaviour. This is a general issue, but of specific relevance to the South China Sea, where the US has been outspoken on the legality of its position on free rights of passage for military assets within an EEZ, including assets engaged in surveillance. It is partly in recognition of the lack of rules governing this relationship, and partly due to the unresolved disagreement on permissible activities within an EEZ, that the US continues to push for some sort of agreement on 'incidents at sea', which could help manage the consequences of any encounters between the assorted militaries and paramilitaries patrolling this sea.

This is a concept that has a clear historical precedent: in 1972, the US and USSR signed an Agreement on the Prevention of Incidents On And Over the High Seas (usually referred to as INCSEA). The agreement attempted to prevent situations where naval vessels may be entangled in escalatory situations. It provided, amongst other initiatives, clear rules to avoid collision: ensuring that surface-borne vessels were informed when submarines were exercising near them, outlawing simulated attacks, and prohibiting the launching of objects towards, or the illumination of bridges on, vessels of the other party. The agreement not only encouraged dialogue between the US and USSR through an annual review, but also reassured commanders that the riskiest behaviours that could easily be misconstrued would be avoided (submarine exercises, for instance, are easy to misread given the inherent clandestine nature of the vessel).

Of obvious potential utility in the South China Sea, China has so far rejected the idea of a Sino-US INCSEA as too reminiscent of the Cold War: this is not the kind of agreement supposed partners should be making. However, without such an agreement, it is reasonable to believe that misunderstandings and unnecessary concerns are likely to arise and, while an INCSEA does not remove the possibility of accidents and collisions, it would surely encourage commanders in the heat of the moment to consider accident as a motive as well as intent.

Removed from its military messaging, the US has also been studiously and repeatedly employing careful diplomatic language in the referencing of the management of territorial and maritime disputes in the South China Sea. With regard to the substance of the claims themselves, it maintains a careful and consistent position of studied neutrality. As Panetta argued at the 2012 Shangri-La Dialogue, 'We call for restraint and for diplomatic resolution; we oppose provocation; we oppose coercion; and we oppose the use of force. We do not take sides when it comes to competing territorial claims, but we do want this dispute resolved peacefully and in a manner consistent with international law.'[38] Despite Chinese intimations to the contrary, the US is clear that it is not trying to insert itself as a mediator in these disputes, but rather as a supporter and enforcer of international norms for acceptable behaviour in dispute resolution.

Nevertheless, through its demands for a collaborative approach and for the clarification of claims, the US is adopting a political line, albeit obliquely. In addition, by supplying vessels and arms to the Philippines, Washington is arguably providing the means for Manila to defend its claims, thereby implicitly supporting the Philippines' position. At the same time, while the US has also deliberately and repeatedly sought to include China in discussions, underlining its support for an inclusive multilateralism which attempts to promote cooperation between ASEAN and China, it has not shied away from focusing specifically on Chinese behaviour with regard to these disputes, for example in repeated critical resolutions in the US Senate.[39]

## Strategic balancing

The states of Southeast Asia are not the only ones involved in a delicate game of strategic balancing. Washington, too, has diverse interests to calibrate. It will, for example, be considering how forcefully and visibly to pursue in the South China Sea its interpretation of military freedoms of navigation provided by UNCLOS. This involves calculating both the contribution such activities make to the broader picture it is collating of China's military build-up, as well as the potential implications for similar activities by the US elsewhere in the world. Washington will also be considering how far it should go in accommodating the interests of a militarily and economically more powerful China within the region, including with particular regard to the South China Sea. Whilst American fundamental tenets and red lines are clear – nations should resolve these disputes without coercion, intimidation or the use of force – incidents such as China's establishment of Sansha City and its associated garrison offer a reminder of the considerable interpretive grey zone that exists around areas of administrative modernisation or economic diplomacy. Finally, Washington will also be thinking about how far it can take its expanding relations with Southeast Asia, which are aimed at shoring up within the region both the US presence, and more obliquely its values. Push too hard, too fast, and potential partners could be alienated. Push too little, or perhaps more realistically, too inconsistently, and potential partners will fret over the long-term credibility of US commitments, with a consequent negative impact for US influence in the region.

This is a balancing act that isn't always easy to get right. As Clinton's impromptu reference to the South China Sea as the 'West Philippine Sea' during a press conference in Manila in 2012 showed, moments of unscripted enthusiasm for closer relations with partners can confuse the picture.[40] Knowing when to pass judgement, and on what, is an art rather than a science. In August of the same year, the strong statement issued by the US State Department on the establishment of Sansha City and its garrison, attracted some critical attention, most predictably but not exclusively from China.[41] The Chinese Foreign Ministry criticised the 'selective approach' shown in this 'so-called statement', which indicated 'a total disregard of facts, confounded right and wrong, and sent a seriously wrong message'.[42] Chinese protests were met in some quarters, even of the US, with cautious sympathy. When the US was anxiously trying to convince China that its interests in the South China Sea were not all a pretext for containing China, why call out China for behaviour none too dissimilar to that already indulged in by other claimants?

Of course, the answer is always the same – fairly or unfairly, and whether China likes it or not, its sheer size and reach mean the consequences of its indulgences in more assertive, and indeed arguably menacing, behaviour will always be greater than the still irresponsible but less meaningful preening exhibited by other smaller and less powerful protagonists.

Nevertheless, the experience provided an important reminder of the challenge the US faces in framing its interests in the South China Sea and responses to developments therein in ways that ensure that Southeast Asian nations continue to be broadly desirous of greater US military, political and economic involvement in their region. Whilst repeated disavowals that the Asia 'pivot' is all about China have generally received short shrift in Beijing, these reminders of US interests in a world beyond Beijing are important within Southeast Asia. These nations are generally receptive to a greater US presence in the region, but they remain divided on the extent to which this should be focused on China and the nature of any great power accommodation that could yet come to pass. For example, whilst historical suspicions may run deep between Vietnam and China, the former will have little enthusiasm for a defence partnership overtly focused on containing China. Statements such as that made in Panetta's speech at the 2012 Shangri-La Dialogue provide important reassurance, not simply to China but also to a Southeast Asia which understandably wants to remain in control of its own destiny: 'China also has a critical role to play in advancing security and prosperity by respecting the rules-based order that has served the region for six decades. The United States welcomes the rise of a strong and prosperous and successful China that plays a greater role in global affairs.'[43]

Ultimately, Southeast Asian states and China alike need to feel confident that the US has little interest in provocation. The South China Sea provides all parties with a diplomatic challenge within an increasingly militarised arena where there is already too much room for perceived provocation. Instability looms large, whether in the mirrors of action–reaction dynamics, in the unpredictable consequences of increasingly frequent skirmishes at sea, or in the differing perceptions of accountability and culpability that result. Perhaps, then, the most comforting thought that can be offered is that, should those involved succeed in finding their way through this particular set of challenges, this very achievement and the resolution it would bring, would radically alter for the better the broader prospects for regional stability.[44]

## Notes

1   Peter A. Dutton, 'Cracks in the Global Foundation: International Law and Instability in the South China Sea', in Cronin (ed.) *Cooperation from Strength*, p. 69.

2   Obama referred to himself as the 'first Pacific President' in a speech to 1,500 prominent Japanese during his state visit to Japan, 14 November 2009. Available at: http://www.whitehouse.gov/the-press-office/remarks-president-barack-obama-suntory-hall.

3   'Pivot to the Pacific? The Obama Administration's "Rebalancing" towards Asia', Congressional Research Service, 28 March 2012, p. 6.

4   See, for example, the speech by President Obama on 14 November 2009 during his state visit to Japan.

5   Former Senator James Webb, in 2012 when he was still chair of the Senate Foreign Relations Sub-Committee on East Asia and Pacific Affairs, quoted in: Craig Whitlock, 'Philippines May Allow Greater US Military Presence in Reaction to China's Rise', *Washington Post*, 25 January 2012, http://www.washingtonpost.com/world/national-security/philippines-may-allow-greater-us-presence-in-latest-reaction-to-chinas-rise/2012/01/24/gIQAhFIyQQ_story_1.html.

6   Tom Donilon, 'America is Back in the Pacific and will Uphold the Rules', *Financial Times*, 27 November 2011, http://www.ft.com/cms/s/0/4f3febac-1761-11e1-b00e-00144feabdc0.html.

7   For a history of *Cobra Gold*, see 'Cobra Gold: A Look at 25 Years of History', US Army Pacific. Http://www.usarpac.army.mil/pdfs/Cobra_Gold_25th.pdf.

8   Although according to the US Pacific Command, annual bilateral naval exchanges between the US and Vietnam are 'CARAT like'. See: James Holmes, 'Rough Waters for Coalition Building', in Cronin (ed.), *Cooperation from Strength*, p. 105.

9   'A Cooperative Strategy for 21st century Seapower', US Navy, US Marine Corps and US Coast Guard,

October 2007, http://www.navy.mil/maritime/Maritimestrategy.pdf.

10  An Dien, 'UXO Decontamination in Vietnam an Uphill Task', *Tanh Nien Weekly*, 9 December 2011.

11  Thayer, 'Hanoi and the Pentagon: A Budding Courtship', USNI, http://news.usni.org/news-analysis/hanoi-and-pentagon-budding-courtship.

12  Although this was down on the US$50m the Philippines received in 2003, when the focus was more on battling al-Qaeda-linked militants. The Philippines' decline in its relative share of US Foreign Military Financing has therefore been the subject of some protest by Manila. Manuel Mogato, 'US Triples Military Aid to the Philippines in 2012', Reuters, 3 May 2012, http://www.reuters.com/article/2012/05/03/us-philippines-usa-idUSBRE8420IU20120503.

13  Whitlock, 'Philippines May Allow Greater US Military Presence in Reaction to China's Rise'.

14  Gidget Fuentes, 'Marines Poised for More Philippine Tours', *Marine Corps Times*, 8 April 2012, http://www.marinecorpstimes.com/news/2012/04/marine-more-philippines-tours-040812/.

15  The ASBC aims to 'defeat, disrupt and destroy' A2AD capabilities by developing closer activities between aerial and naval units of the armed forces and hence ensure continued freedom of manoeuvre for the US in the Western Pacific. It may prove too bellicose to be used, however, as it potentially suggests deep strikes into Chinese territory at the outset of hostilities. For a fuller analysis, see: 'New US Military Concept Marks Pivot to Sea and Air', IISS *Strategic Comments*, vol. 18, no. 20, May 2012.

16  A2AD capabilities, in the guise of fast attack craft with anti-ship missiles, submarines and anti-ship ballistic missiles, attempt first to prevent the entry of an adversary into a theatre of operations and then to complicate the adversary's ability to operate in this theatre.

17  Joint Operational Access Concept, US Department of Defence, 17 January 2012. Available at: http://www.defense.gov/pubs/pdfs/JOAC_Jan%202012_Signed.pdf.

18  For a description of the US military posture and strategy, see: Christian Le Mière, 'America's Pivot to East Asia: The Naval Dimension'.

19  There was, however, some outreach, for example with the boosting of political and economic relations with Indonesia and Malaysia. Some of the groundwork for the eventual US accession to the EAS was also done under the G.W. Bush administration.

20  Julie Pace, 'Obama Makes History with Myanmar, Cambodia Visits', Associated Press, 20 November 2012.

21  Joint Statement of 2nd US–ASEAN Leaders Meeting. For full text, see: http://newasiarepublic.com/?p=20848.

22  For more details on US input into the debate on maritime security, see 'Fact Sheet: East Asia Summit', The White House Office of the Press Secretary, 19 November 2011, http://www.whitehouse.gov/the-press-office/2011/11/19/fact-sheet-east-asia-summit.

23 Leon Panetta, 'The US Rebalance towards the Asia Pacific', speech at the Shangri-La Dialogue, Singapore, 2 June 2012.

24 Interview with a US observer of South China Sea dynamics, Shangri-La Dialogue, Singapore, June 2012.

25 'Cambodia's Garment Exports to US Support at least 1.8 Million people', *Khmerization*, 20 January 2012, http://khmerization.blogspot. de/2012/01/cambodias-garment-exports-to-us-support.html.

26 Demetrios J. Marantis, 'The Obama Administration's Asia-Pacific Trade Policy', speech at the Washington Council on International Trade, July 2012. Available at: http://www.ustr. gov/about-us/press-office/speeches/ transcripts/2012/july.

27 For more details on US trade relations with ASEAN, see the record on recent developments with ASEAN on the website of the Office of the US Trade Representative in the Executive Office of the President: http://www.ustr.gov/ countries-regions/southeast-asia-pacific/association-southeast-asian-nations-asean.

28 *Ibid.*

29 Thomas Donnelly, 'Recycling "Reset"', *The Weekly Standard* blog, 25 October 2011, http:// www.weeklystandard.com/blogs/ recycling-reset_603991.html.

30 Panetta, 'The US Rebalance towards the Asia Pacific'.

31 Tim Huxley, 'PacNet Number 35R', Pacific Forum CSIS, Honolulu, 12 June 2012, http://csis.org/files/ publication/Pac1235R.pdf.

32 Dutton, 'Cracks in the Global Foundation: International Law and Instability in the South China Sea', p. 74.

33 Quoted in: Josh Rogin, 'New Push Beings for Law of the Sea Treaty', The Cable, *Foreign Policy*, 10 May 2012.

34 This point was made by Gideon Rachman with reference to disputes between Japan and China over the Senkakus/Diaoyu islands in 2012, in: 'The Risk of US–China Conflict', *Financial Times*, 22 August 2012.

35 Chinese Defence Ministry Spokesman Senior Colonel Geng Yansheng, cited in: 'Pivot to the Pacific? The Obama Administration's "Rebalancing" towards Asia', Congressional Research Service, 28 March 2012, p. 19.

36 *Ibid.*, p. 18.

37 See, for example, Gates's speech and comments at the Shangri-La Dialogue, June 2011.

38 Panetta, 'The US Rebalance towards the Asia-Pacific'.

39 See, for example, the Senate Resolution of June 2011 (Resolution 217) deploring the use of force by China in the South China Sea, and a further resolution (524) of August 2012 declaring that China's recent actions with regard to Sansha 'impede a peaceful resolution'.

40 This is the name for the South China Sea used in official Philippine correspondence since June 2011. Clinton's statement appeared to undermine US claims to neutrality but were likely simply a slip of the tongue.

41 Statement by Patrick Ventrell, acting deputy spokesman, State Department, on 3 August 2012. Available at: http://www.state.gov/r/ pa/prs/ps/2012/08/196022.htm.

42 Full statement available in English at http://www.fmprc.gov.cn/eng/xwfw/s2510/t958226.htm.

43 Panetta, 'The US Rebalance towards the Asia-Pacific'.

44 For a version of this argument, see: James Dobbins, 'War with China', *Survival*, vol. 54, no. 4, August–September 2012, pp. 7–24. Dobbins argues that coping successfully with smaller challenges might be one of the best ways of ensuring that China and the US don't need to fight a larger war.

This *Adelphi* has focused on tracking and unpacking the disputes within the South China Sea in the belief that these offer a potential crucible for the unfolding geopolitics of Southeast Asia. These disputes hold geopolitical significance not simply with regard to their eventual outcome, but also as concerns the very process of their management towards resolution. As China, Southeast Asian nations and the US all seek to influence dynamics surrounding the sea, and as other nations in the region, including India, Japan, South Korea and Australia become more involved, so the handling of these disputes is set significantly to influence the evolving balance of power in the region, and perhaps even the prospects for peace in the Asia-Pacific in the twenty-first century.

The potential centrality of the South China Sea disputes to these prospects for peace is perhaps best illustrated by the sketching of four broad scenarios through which tensions in the sea might inform and influence the future development of Southeast Asian relations and the emerging regional order. By nature of their generality, all the scenarios are to some extent caricatures of a situation which is likely, in reality, to be more complex and less easily compartmentalised. They are also supported by underlying assumptions which are often, in themselves, contentious. Nevertheless, such an exercise in horizon-scanning can help identify the general trends in development and four such scenarios are therefore offered in this concluding chapter. Consideration is also given to some of the potential way-markers and variables that will influence which scenario is more likely to develop, and, lastly, to some possible policy prescriptions for managing dynamics towards a preferred, peaceful conclusion.

## Mapping the future of the South China Sea
### Scenario 1. Nobody's sea: stable cohabitation

Under this scenario, the US pragmatically – if perhaps reluctantly – accepts the end of the era of its uncontested naval primacy in Asia. Perhaps helped by the mutual reassurances provided for through a complex web of overlapping partnerships with Southeast Asian countries, the dangers of great-power competition and conflict in a nuclear world are rejected in favour of a peaceful new order, built on inclusive cooperation and partnership between the two major powers of the US and China.[1] China would be given what former Australian Prime Minister Paul Keating has referred to as 'the strategic space' to rise to clear regional prominence, if not dominance.[2] The situation would therefore be one of wary stability through voluntary restraint: the US would withdraw to some extent from Southeast Asia (although not the western Pacific) but China would not be powerful or confident enough to effect a total US abandonment or assume the position as *primus inter pares*.[3] Some Southeast Asian states would be more comfortable than others with this rebalancing, but in short, no one state would dominate the South China Sea.

With particular regard to the maritime disputes, competing claims on territorial sovereignty and maritime rights could conceivably continue between China and Southeast Asian states, but the US would be content that China in particular was willing to address these differences through peaceful means, with full respect for established international law. Differences between the US and China over freedom of navigation for military vessels within an EEZ would either be resolved or at least shelved by mutual consent and restraint.

An agreement, for example on joint development between rival claimants or around EEZ rights of passage between the US and China, could be a key contributor to the emergence of such a stable cooperative scenario, removing as it would obvious points of friction in the South China Sea. Alternatively, the impetus for a more collaborative partnership between China and the US in particular could be found elsewhere – for example following a breakthrough on the Korean peninsula or over the future of Taiwan. In this scenario, the South China Sea and prospects for stability therein would be the beneficiary of, as opposed to the catalyst to, such broader cooperation.

Either way, several key underlying assumptions would have to be met. The US would have to be persuaded to take a more consultative approach, accepting some undermining of its fundamental premise of primacy, on which its sea-strategy in Asia has been based for the past two hundred years. Indeed, this would be a departure from the past half-millennium of activity in the region whereby, as US Naval War College Associate Professor James Holmes has noted, 'a single dominant sea power – first Portugal, then Holland, then Great Britain and finally the United States – has provided maritime security'.[4] Such a shift in thinking in the US could be forced by economic constraints, or be reflective of a more theoretical change in outlook that was perhaps simply less global in its demands and more willing to power-share with regional partners. Underlying issues of concern, most crucially over the intent behind China's military build-up, would have to have been addressed, likely in part by greater Chinese transparency on these issues.

Yet even if these assumptions were to prove to be correct, such a condominium would bring its own set of challenges for Southeast Asia and would certainly prove problematic for established US allies in Northeast Asia. Whilst Southeast Asian nations have the capacity to play a brokering role in the emergence of such a condominium, they would surely be concerned that too close a partnership between the bigger powers of the US and China could come at the expense of their own strategic autonomy. It is perhaps for this very reason that states such as Vietnam and the Philippines are supportive of an internationalisation of these disputes that extends beyond the US to include others such as India, Australia and Japan. The continued rise of China, combined with the perception of a US willing to afford Beijing more strategic space, would also likely bring consequences for Northeast Asia's defence procurement postures and political stability. Economic travails notwithstanding, Tokyo, for example, would be incentivised to develop its defence capabilities more rapidly in order to withstand any perceived Chinese threat.

Meanwhile, an 'entente pragmatique' between the US and China in the South China Sea would not necessarily bring any impetus for a resolution of the island disputes themselves. Indeed, given continued involvement by the US in the region and the interest of most Southeast Asian states in sustaining these interactions at some level, it would still seem unlikely either that China would be able to coerce regional states into an agreement or that other claimants would consider ceding their positions. As such, the disputes would be likely to fester, even whilst the possibility of great-power conflict over them would dissipate.

### Scenario 2. Somebody's sea: regional hegemony

Under this scenario, one regional hegemon establishes itself as the unrivalled regional naval power and protector of freedom of navigation through the South China Sea. In the instance that this power was China, the parallel US retreat to the Western Pacific could come either through a conscious choice that would flow, for example, from acute budgetary pressures, a recurrent bout of relative isolationism, or substantial foreign-policy disturbances closer to home. It could also come about through the exercise of force, affected in such a way as to fatefully undermine US willpower to match its rhetoric with action in the region.

Such a scenario hinges on the assumption that China continues to rise, further increasing its influence in its neighbourhood, with domestic stability ensured through continued economic growth. It necessarily entails the avoidance of any 'landing' for China's economy, whether hard or soft.

Within the South China Sea, whilst the Headquarters of the South Sea Fleet at Zhanjiang would continue to be a major naval base, in particular for Chinese surface ships, the Yulin naval base on Hainan would likely become the key regional base for the projection of influence, with primary responsibility for protecting sea lines of communication. China would have seen off the US challenge on rights to military surveillance within its EEZ, although not necessarily through any codified reinterpretation of UNCLOS – since, in this scenario China, might now find such rights of surveillance, as previously promoted by the US and others, useful for retaining its own newly established position of regional hegemony. Yet even with the removal of the bigger strategic imperative supporting its claims in the South China Sea, China would likely remain committed to its territorial and maritime claims in the South China Sea, motivated in part by continuing rising domestic demand for hydrocarbons and fisheries and backed by its now established hard-power superiority. The choice between a more conciliatory or more aggressive pursuit of these claims would be China's to make, with minimal consideration given to external constraints. Should China stay true to its rhetoric, a more cooperative and collaborative approach to the sea's resources could perhaps be imagined between claimant countries, but this would be pursued from an even clearer position of strength than at present, since China's partners in any such venture would be in no doubt where influence ultimately lay.

In broader terms, such a scenario of 'Pax Sinica' has implications for the region in terms of the values that will dominate, including prospects for democracy and interpretations of international law. Although by no means predetermined to evolve in this fashion, Southeast Asian nations would at the very least be wary about the possibility of finding themselves operating under a modern-day or virtual tributary system – which was the norm for so much of their historical dealings with imperial China.[5] Economic inducement and military protection might well on occasion be provided, but the price would be regular compliance with Chinese interests and demands.

Alternatively under this scenario, it would be the US that would re-establish itself as the unchallenged power and provider of global public goods in Asia, including with regard to the South China Sea. This would likely reflect a 'hard landing' for China's economy, leading to some sort of internal unrest which brought to an end, at least for the foreseeable future, either China's ability or desire for increased influence over the environment beyond its borders. Yet it could also be that the South China Sea has a role to play in the precipitation of this alternative – for example through Chinese miscalculation over the force with which it pursues its territorial or maritime claims, which leads in turn to an escalatory clash that results in the clear defeat of Chinese interests in the South China Sea. Such a defeat would not necessarily have to go so far even as to involve the surrender of features already occupied by China, let alone a more dramatic collapse of order on the mainland, but it would at a minimum mark the end of claims centred on the nine-dashed line and the end of any further militarisation of features already occupied by China. US-led broader interpretations of freedom of navigation entitlements would be clearly established, with Chinese naval ambitions likewise kept firmly in check.

Whilst such an alternative might also improve the prospects for stability in the South China Sea – although it would still not resolve the issue of competing sovereignty claims between the remaining five claimants – neighbouring states in Southeast Asia and beyond are unlikely to find much comfort in such a scenario. They rightly fear the possible consequences of any precipitate and substantive breakdown of stability in China as much, and perhaps more, than the implications of its continued rise.

### Scenario 3. Everybody's sea: managed mistrust

Under this scenario, the US continues as the leading naval power in the region and key provider of global public goods. Chinese naval capabilities continue to grow, and its interests in territorial, maritime and even EEZ claims remain unbowed. Yet these potentially conflicting dynamics are managed in ways that ensure they are underpinned by a platform of stability and predictability. International law would take centre stage in the management of disputes, with tensions in the South China Sea no longer serving as a potential flashpoint in the management of regional rivalries, but rather as a model for what dialogue and confidence-building measures can achieve. Nonetheless, regional states would likely continue to hedge by investing in increasingly advanced military equipment, often with a clear view to deter specific rivals, underlining the action–reaction dynamics of the procurement processes. The South China Sea would continue to be a zone of latent antagonism, but one where negotiation runs in parallel with military procurement, helping to prevent a slide into conflict.

Key assumptions underpinning this scenario include a belated move by China to clarify its claims under UNCLOS, thereby giving all involved – no matter how indirectly – the confidence that China is willing to manage its ambitions within the bounds of established international law. Southeast Asian nations, perhaps through the collective of ASEAN, would also likely have managed proactively to pursue a coherent approach which successfully enmeshes key actors in the region in a kaleidoscope of power, serving to minimise the interest and ability of one or two great powers to disturb the status quo single-handedly.

One possible result of such successful and stable pragmatism in the South China Sea could be that US–China relations are actually improved, with the confidence developed from the responsible management of this potential flashpoint serving as a useful stepping stone to looking at the management of bigger challenges elsewhere.[6] However, this scenario – which realistically still involves tacit competition between the US and China on the one hand and China and regional states on the other – may well have the appearance of chaotic rivalry. With roles for all actors in the processes of conflict management and resolution (from China to individual Southeast Asian states, ASEAN and the US), the dynamic in the sea would be one of disorderly but stable contest.

## Scenario 4. Sea of conflict

Whilst the first three scenarios outlined for the South China Sea could all theoretically, though not necessarily, come about through peaceful means, this fourth and final scenario is both a scenario in its own right, and also of course a potential launch pad for onwards transition to one of the first three scenarios. However, the potential consequences of this fourth scenario are sufficiently dire and diverse that predictions on the actual outcome cannot sensibly be made, and it is therefore outlined as a standalone scenario in its own right.

Under this scenario, there exist four possible conflicts, separated between two different variables. The conflict would be either planned or unplanned, and involve, initially, either China and the US or China and a Southeast Asian state. In either variable, anything more than the shortest conflict would be likely to draw in other actors as well, both in the immediate region and beyond. Whilst conflict remains unlikely, some variants of this scenario are more probable than others.

In the case of a planned conflict, one possible variant is that one of the more significant powers, namely either the US or China, decides to enforce their will on the region through military power. This is the least probable of the variants since, at least in the short to medium term, neither the US nor China are likely to perceive an advantage to the deliberate, first-use, direct-deployment of their hard-power capabilities. In the case of the US, such actions would critically undercut their claims to be a force for regional stability. On the other hand, such aggressive actions on the part of their primary regional challenger, China, would severely undermine the country's doctrine of 'peaceful rise', while confirming the worst suspicions of an already mistrustful neighbourhood. Yet, it is not just concerns over image that would deter a descent into significant conflict: the size of armed forces ranged against each other and the costs involved in any conflict, particularly given the possibility of further escalation, act as a substantial deterrent in their own right. Even though US forces in aggregate are far superior to those of China, the PLA would benefit from the geographical advantage of proximity to the South China Sea, making it less necessary to refuel aircraft in air and allowing for the utilisation of a broader range of vessels. It is unlikely that either side would be able to limit any conflict to a brief naval engagement, whether motivated by, for example, Washington's interest in demonstrating to Beijing that the US remained the regional hegemon, or, alternatively, Beijing's wish to send a message to the US that China intends to become the primary arbiter of security in its own neighbourhood. Of course, in this variant, the initial military outcome, if not the subsequent diplomatic wrangling, would depend upon the assets involved.

There is, however, a more probable version of a planned 'conflict scenario': a weaker military power in the neighbourhood might conceivably attempt to use its military to defend its territorial claims, from, for example, exploratory activities by Chinese vessels, supported by their paramilitary agencies, within the EEZ of the weaker state. In this case, the initial escalation to a military footing could be painted by the weaker power as 'defensive'. The hope would be that their actions could be justifiable under international law and that any subsequent retaliation or escalation by China would confirm Beijing's underlying role as the aggressor. However, given the potentially devastating consequences for the weaker party, this would be a high-risk policy. Indeed, much of the investment in naval capabilities among the Southeast Asian states, from submarines to anti-ship missiles and fast-attack craft, has been largely defensive in nature, focused on deterring and perhaps defeating a Chinese attack in the short term alone. In the medium term, the reality is that any individual Southeast

Asian nations would be easily overwhelmed militarily by the superiority of Chinese assets.

More credible perhaps would be a calculated first use of force by Beijing, with the launch of a deliberate but brief strike on a Southeast Asian nation's defences or fortifications in the South China Sea. With the advantage of superior technology and precision-guided, stand-off weaponry, China could hope to deliver a sharp burst of violence on a lesser-armed opponent aimed at degrading their defensive capabilities and asserting Beijing's military dominance. Alternatively, a managed campaign could attempt to oust one nation from a particular position or set of positions on the features of the South China Sea, swiftly followed by a Chinese occupation and fortification, in an action reminiscent of the Battle of the Paracels in 1974.

Importantly, such a planned campaign need not necessarily be intended just to gain tactical advantage in the sea; the dispute could instead be used as an outlet for violence that is primarily driven by otherwise unrelated policies and events. In this sense, the South China Sea becomes not just a crucible for regional and great power competition but also a potential conduit for the consequences of that competition.

However, one further aspect that mitigates against the likelihood of a planned conflict scenario involving China and Southeast Asia, in which China would be the first to deploy force, is the possibility of such actions attracting the involvement of the US. In the case of an attack on a Southeast Asian state, and in particular on an ally of the US such as the Philippines, Washington's response would be key both to the result and to the future order of the region. If the US stepped in to the dispute promptly and decisively, through the calibrated and proportionate deployment of a military as well as a diplomatic response, and was able to contain any conflict before it had a chance to escalate further, then Beijing would likely be defeated and indeed militarily embarrassed, suggesting a return to the status quo ante of a dominant US in the South China Sea. Alternatively, if a war-weary US procrastinated and was perceived to waver in its commitment to the region, uncertainty and instability would be likely to spread. This could result in a quick 'win' for China – at least on a military if not a broader diplomatic level – as regional states failed to find the unity of action that would be required to face down Chinese aggression. However, it could also lead to a messy fracturing of the region into a range of responses that would serve to complicate, and perhaps even conflagrate, the unfolding conflict.

In the second, and more probable, version of this scenario, conflict breaks out by accident rather than by design. Most likely it begins with a clash between China and a Southeast Asian nation, with tensions in the South China Sea proving unmanageable through diplomatic or legal channels. An accident at sea between competing paramilitaries quickly becomes an incident at sea as it is badly handled in its early stages. This incident escalates thanks to the actions of the paramilitary and naval officers involved, who respond to events in ways which quickly curtail options for their responsible management higher up the command chain. The death of a sailor or the inadvertent damage to, and potential sinking of, a ship as an unintended consequence would only make this scenario more emotional and problematic.

Alternatively, a miscalculation could be made by one or more claimants as to the extent to which they have licence to push their claims before triggering an unexpectedly robust response, forcing action–reaction dynamics into the military realm. Warning shots or aggressive manoeuvres could be misinterpreted if the rules of engagement are either not clearly established or are poorly transmitted, leading to reactive escalation. Worse still, casualties could easily be interpreted as a *casus belli* – a form of accidental Gulf of Tonkin or USS *Maine* incident (both instances where perceived attacks against US naval assets led to greater US dedication to a conflict, the former in Vietnam and the latter in the Spanish–American War). Either way, popular nationalism in the claimant states and potentially the US would prove an important accelerant on the path to conflict. It would allow a seemingly small initial incident to acquire an escalatory momentum of its own, towards a violent conflagration which no party initially intended or desired. Yet too quickly, too much would be perceived to be at stake by those now engaged in this inadvertent stand-off to offer alternative pathways to resolution aside from conflict. For the Asian participants in such a drama, regime credibility would likely be at stake, possibly through the backlash of the ballot box at subsequent elections were the respective government perceived to have failed to protect territorial integrity. Or, in the case of China, through the backlash of the blogosphere where uncontrolled nationalist sentiment would quickly paint a picture of a Communist Party that had abandoned its economic principles in favour of crony capitalism and had now betrayed the 'unification' credentials it has claimed for itself since 1949 and the ending of the Chinese Civil War.

The early participants in any such occurrence of conflict by accident or miscalculation would vary according to the specifics of the initial incident, but the nature of the overlapping claims and the principles that would be at stake would likely draw in others quickly. For example, in perhaps the most likely of the options under this conflict scenario, if the initial incident were to involve a miscalculated assertion of will concerning territorial or maritime rights, which in turn attracted an unexpectedly robust response, conflict would begin between two claimants but likely escalate to involve others, including perhaps a non-claimant in the form of the US. On the other hand, if the initial incident were to centre more on disputes over freedom of navigation in EEZs, it is more likely to involve the US and China at the outset – thanks, for example, to a poorly managed accidental collision between US surveillance vessels operating inside China's EEZ and Chinese vessels seeking to limit the scope of such activities. In the stand-off that could credibly ensue, Southeast Asian nations would quickly be caught in a middle that they have long sought to avoid.

Once again, for any conflict to be truly damaging at a strategic level, it would need to escalate to the point of at least engaging the US in a decision as to whether or not to get involved. It might be that the US ultimately decides against any need for military (as opposed to diplomatic) engagement – for example in the event of a contained military clash between two claimant states over island claims or drilling rights. In this instance, the escalatory nature of the conflict *might* therefore be limited. However, even if this did transpire to be the case, this would not necessarily mean that the strategic consequences would be similarly limited. Once violence has been deployed, in particular if it is perceived as emanating from the emerging regional power of China against the smaller and medium-sized powers of Southeast Asia, then a US decision *not* to engage potentially impacts the future regional order as much as a decision *to* engage. Either way, the US finds itself with an unenviable choice: honouring actual or perceived security commitments (for example in the 1951 Mutual Defence Treaty it has signed with the Philippines) and thereby engaging in a conflict not existential to its own security interests; or, opting out with the consequent reputational damage to the credibility of the security umbrella it purports to provide.[7]

Disconcertingly, when it comes to measuring the likelihood of the different variants under this conflict scenario, inherent to them are many of the assumptions and dynamics that we already see in evidence today. For example, pressures on hydrocarbon and fishery resources continue to mount, increasing the stakes for claimant countries. Likewise, the US and China continue to appear uneasy with each other's naval ambitions and strategic requirements, with action–reaction dynamics evident, for example, in the development of the ASBC as one answer to Chinese efforts to develop credible A2AD strategies. Meanwhile, concerns continue to run high within the region and beyond over a perceived lack of transparency over Chinese military capabilities and the intent behind their development. Rules of engagement, similarly, remain unclear, while formal procedures for incidents at sea are yet to be established. Perhaps most disconcertingly of all, however, is that rising domestic nationalism on all sides of the sea is intermingling with government populism to increase the danger of the tail wagging the dog.

The implications for such a scenario of conflict are radical, but unclear and unpredictable. The only sensible analysis that can be offered here is that this is a die which no power wants to have to roll and which is unlikely to be in the interests of many, or indeed any.

## Identifying way markers

Before turning to examine possible policy proposals that could help manage the negative dynamics presently unfolding in the South China Sea and their impact on the evolving regional order, it is worth first highlighting a few key issues to watch which could help policymakers and shapers assess not just what might happen, or should happen, but what is actually happening. To this end, five crucial variables are now presented, the first three of which are focused on behaviours by the key leaderships involved.

## i) The role of China's leadership

As the CCP, under the curatorship of its fifth generation of leaders, seeks to navigate its way through tensions within the party, between the party and society, and between the country and its neighbourhood, it faces a balancing act in deciding how far and how hard to push its interests in the management of these disputes.

Although the prospects for the pivotal role of a single charismatic leader have reduced considerably since the days of Mao and Deng, a strong collective leadership, confident in its military capabilities and in its calculations of an ability to deploy these with limited retribution, might logically view increased assertiveness in the South China Sea as an attractive option, or at least a test case, for power projection. After all, part of the reason that the disputes are so complicated to resolve is that the stakes are so high. In other words, a more confident China might be more resolute about pushing to secure these stakes. It could also be yet more strategic in its approach. China's leadership has, for example, long been reluctant to enter into substantive negotiations on a Code of Conduct, despite a long-standing commitment to this effect in the 2002 DoC. However, a more confident Chinese leadership could credibly decide this was an area where controlled progress towards a code that was no more than modestly ambitious could actually improve China's operational environment rather than restrict it. China would simply need to engage sufficiently so as to satisfy underlying concerns with regard to freedom of navigation. It could, in the process, conveniently undercut a key lever of regional engagement presently in US hands.

The alternative variable of a continued dilution of legitimacy within the CCP leadership, with the necessary compromises of collective leadership resulting in a weaker rather than a stronger base, is however perhaps more likely. Yet weak Chinese

leadership (whether as a short-term result of a new government feeling the need to prove its credentials to its people, or
as a more medium-term result of increasing instability inside
China) also carries with it the dangers of adventurism, as the
government seeks a unifying cause with which to divert the
attentions of its people. Indeed, China has previously utilised
violence in its territorial disputes overseas when it has perceived
adversaries as attempting to profit from the country's internal
difficulties, namely with India in 1962 and the Soviet Union
in 1969. Since its establishment in 1949, China has resolved 17
border disputes through negotiation and compromise, some of
them at the height of internal trauma, but it has also preferred
to use violence to prevent a weakening of its position in any
dispute or in regional relations and has rarely compromised on
territorial issues that have strategic consequences.[9] The possibility of the use of violence amid domestic ructions over the
South China Sea therefore remains.

Confident or weak, Beijing's leadership has a difficult task
keeping the party's diversifying factions and interest groups
content inside one tent. The continuation of its present balancing
act of regular reassuring rhetoric interspersed with occasional
assertive demonstrations of intent is a complex and perhaps
ultimately irreconcilable challenge. Yet its success in managing such demands will be a key factor in fashioning Southeast
Asia's response to China's rise and, with it, US prospects for its
own balancing act in the region.

## ii) The role of ASEAN leadership

As this book has argued, individual nation states in Southeast
Asia have an important role to play in the development of relations between the US and China with regard to the South China
Sea. Yet, even with the most proactive and effective diplomacy,
there is a limit to the influence smaller and medium-sized

powers can have on larger powers. One utility of multilateral diplomacy, however, is that it extends this limit, in part by placing smaller nations on an equal footing with larger nations. Especially within a consensus-driven institution, a vote is a vote. And so, although ASEAN may remain very much a work in progress – and slow progress at that – in any assessment of scenarios that may unfold around the South China Sea, ASEAN's evolution should be carefully watched.

A disunited ASEAN is more likely to embed great-power dominance in the regional strategic dynamic. On the other hand, a more influential, if not united ASEAN, playing an active role in the development of broader regional security architecture including the East Asia Summit, is more likely to be able to prosecute the enmeshment strategies its individual member states have been developing. Effective multilateralism in Asia would make a substantive contribution towards the management of China's rise, increasing the chances of stability, and in a manner that would force bigger powers to take note of regional concerns whilst avoiding any temptation to ride roughshod over them.

Meanwhile, the activities of individual Southeast Asian nations are, of course, important in the development of the disputes themselves. For example, one driver of recent Chinese assertiveness has been more activity in hydrocarbon exploration by Vietnam and the Philippines in the South China Sea. Furthermore, defence procurement processes by regional states may not make a substantial impact on the broader balance of power, but, by creating a sense of military rivalry, they certainly influence the atmosphere in which diplomacy takes place.

### iii) The role of US leadership
The US has an important role to play as a key restraining influence in the South China Sea, in particular on Chinese behaviour.

Where US leadership has appeared weak or wanting – perhaps distracted by events elsewhere – the unintentional result has been the indirect encouragement of greater Chinese assertiveness. This was true in China's seizure of the remaining half of the Paracels in 1974, and it was again reflected in China's increasingly robust assertions of sovereignty during the latter half of the first decade of the twenty-first century, at a time when the US was preoccupied with Iraq and Afghanistan and talk of American decline was surging.

With the rhetorical commitment to 'showing up' involved in the 'pivot to Asia', American administrations have set themselves a new benchmark against which the sustainability of their commitments to the region will be judged. Repeated failure to participate at the right level in one of the multiple conventions of assorted regional security forums may not, in reality, reflect anything more than US frustration at lack of substantive agendas, but in the shaping of a Southeast Asian regional order, perceptions will matter as much as reality. Is the US really committed for the long run? US officials can declare it is so, but it will be the region's opinions which will ultimately matter, as member states fashion their security policies accordingly.

The degree to which the US is able to exercise subtlety in its regional leadership will also be important in determining future positioning in the region. Overbearing assumptions that the region 'needs' the US, for example to hedge against the rise of China, risk unnecessarily undermining enthusiasm for the US's role in the region. Ultimately, effective US leadership depends on Southeast Asian complicity, which itself flows from a calculation that a US presence is a stabilising and therefore welcome one. Although some degree of tension between China and Southeast Asia might well suit US interests through the creation of a favourable operational environment in which partnership is sought and values debated, too much tension also poses obvious risks for the US, as the ultimate guarantor of security in the region. Similarly, a recklessly emboldened ally, misreading strong US rhetorical support, could also lead the US towards decisions which ultimately prove contrary to its national interests.

There will also need to be evidence of a parallel, consistent and comprehensive outreach by the US towards a rising China. This will provide reassurance, whilst also helping to manage the dangers of action–reaction dynamics through the development of a better mutual appreciation for distinguishing between tactics and underlying strategic intent.

US commitment to meeting the costs of ensuring its 'cooperative primacy' in the South China Sea should also be monitored.[9] Ultimately the US ability to build a broad network of more capable partners in Southeast Asia – a key criteria for meeting its interests in the South China Sea and the region more generally – will have to be underlined by a diplomacy that is more than simply focused on common security interests. More comprehensive relations will need cultivating across the board, including in areas such as trade policy, where US administrations have traditionally encountered domestic problems in pushing forward agendas supportive of their foreign-policy interests. Meanwhile, the US will need to continue to excel at countering Chinese military developments, whether through the innovation of responses to China's A2AD capabilities or the traditional matching of China's growing sea-control capabilities, in order to prevent a restructuring of the strategic balance of power in the region that undermines Washington's security interests.

### iv) The role of the militaries

Given the concern that present trends in the South China Sea point too readily towards Scenario 4 – the advent of conflict, either by accident or design – it is reasonable to suggest that future developments around the sea will also be heavily influenced by the evolution, command and control structures and deployments of regional militaries and paramilitaries. It is for this reason that the practice and promotion of military-military dialogues, in particular between the US and China, are so important. Yet, at times, both states have been willing to cease involvement in such dialogues. In the case of the US, relations were cut for a year after the EP-3 incident over Hainan in 2001, whilst China seems to continue to regard the concession of its involvement in such dialogues as reflective of acceptable political conditions at the time, rather than as the vehicle towards the fashioning of such conditions. As the US leadership decides to sell arms to Taiwan, meet the Dalai Lama or otherwise misbehave in Chinese eyes, so the dialogue stops and starts its way from crisis to crisis.[10]

Moreover, in some states involved in the dispute, such as Vietnam and the Philippines, where civilian control over the military is less well established than in countries such as the US, the independent variable of military conduct is further heightened. However, it is in China where the military's role in decision-making is of paramount importance to the development of the South China Sea disputes. The PLA's influence in policy and its traditionally relatively hardline policy positions mean that the fifth generation's ability to control the military will be key to the development of these disputes. Xi Jinping has solid military experience and credentials, having worked after graduation as a secretary in the Central Military Commission's general office and aide to then Defence Minister Geng Biao, and subsequently as first secretary of the Fujian and Nanjing PLA military regions, as well as director of the National Defence Mobilisation Committee. For the moment, though, it remains unclear whether this experience will afford him greater influence over the PLA, and hence act as a restraint on some of the more hardline opinions emanating from this particular constituency, or whether it will encourage Xi to see things from the military's point of view, thereby amplifying PLA influence in the policymaking machinery.

The actions of paramilitaries (which remain for the present the primary agencies for the enforcement of claims) will also be important, in particular in their management of incidents at sea, as they challenge each other's mandates for operations in contested areas. Likewise, China's helpful preference for deploying 'only' paramilitaries in its shows of force – keeping militarily more capable PLAN vessels over the horizon – needs to be watched. Any move towards a front-line deployment of a PLAN vessel in support of China's claims would send a message to claimants and the region alike which is, by definition, escalatory. In contrast, any moves towards more collaborative cooperation between assorted national paramilitaries – for example with regard to the protection of the maritime environment or on counter-piracy or search-and-rescue missions – will offer more positive indications regarding prospective stability.

### v) The role of populism

The escalatory role of nationalism in the development of maritime disputes could be clearly seen in autumn 2012 in Beijing's management of tensions in the East China Sea. Protests were initially incited by the nationalisation by the government of Japan of three of the uninhabited islands in the disputed Senkaku/Diaoyu Island grouping. However, the context provided a catalyst for anti-Japanese demonstrations: the nationalisation occurred just a week before the 81st anniversary of the Mukden Incident, a false-flag bombing orchestrated by the Imperial Japanese Army to justify a more robust invasion of Manchuria. Moreover, the Japanese purchase of the islands occurred amid the run-up to the 2012 leadership transition in China (following the sensational downfall of prospective Politburo Standing Committee member Bo Xilai) and overlapped in part with the unexplained temporary disappearance from public life of the presumed President-elect Xi Jinping. In such circumstances, Beijing saw little advantage in listening to the protestations of the Japanese government that their move had been a responsible one designed to deescalate disputes through the prevention of a more inflammatory purchase by the nationalist mayor of Tokyo. Instead popular anti-Japanese sentiment was given full vent on the mainland, further fuelling an already unstable situation during which an incident at sea could have potentially resulted in dire consequences, not readily controllable by a government set on staying in power.

Yet, whether in the East or South China Sea, China is far from the only government in the region both simultaneously fuelling and facing the demands of popular nationalism. Vietnam, in particular, is similarly haunted by nationalist sentiment with regard to its claims to the Paracels and Spratlys. Despite their difficult history, China and Vietnam have found compromises over competing land border claims as well as maritime claims in the Gulf of Tonkin, in part because their governments saw advantage in leading from the front and taking on the populist narrative. However, this balance between leadership and following is becoming increasingly complicated in a media age where, even in countries exercising considerable restrictions on personal freedoms, not everything can be as controlled and scripted as before. Social media tools, including microblogs such as China's Weibo sites, can develop their own constituencies with their own arguments, not all of which are consistent with a government's preferred narrative.

Meanwhile governments across the region remain wary of nationalism's twin dangers. These are, namely, that any protests could turn against the government, particularly in countries like China and Vietnam where there is a noticeable lack of other outlets for representation and protest, and that the nationalist discourse can overtake policymaking and force the government into positions it may not wish to retain. It is for these reasons that the Chinese government was assiduous in preventing extended protests in September 2012 over the Senkaku/Diaoyu Islands, despite having first rhetorically and logistically supported them for several days.

The fear remains that governments in these countries (and others, most notably the Philippines) will become hostage to the echoes of the region's long history of enmity, which continues to reverberate through the population at large. According to this narrative, there is a danger that the granting of even the most minor of concessions could become threatening to social stability in a way unappetising to democratically elected and authoritarian governments alike.

## Managing tensions in the South China Sea

Ultimately leaders in China, Southeast Asia and the US will change, militaries will evolve and populism will rise and fall. Yet the underlying strategic geography of the South China Sea will remain.[11] It will continue as a key transit route for trade between east and west. It will still constitute part of China's problematic second island chain and the route out for its blue-water navy to the Indian Ocean and beyond. Even if the sea's oil reserves prove to have been seriously over-estimated, its reserves of gas and fisheries will continue to lend it considerable resource significance within the region. Access to, and indeed primary control over the South China Sea will therefore continue to carry important political, military, economic and resource rewards.

It is in this context that this book concludes with a series of policy proposals aimed at managing these dynamics. Of the four scenarios outlined at the start of this chapter, it is judged that policymakers of all hues are likely to assess Scenario 3 (that of managed mistrust in 'Everybody's sea') as the most pragmatic and realistic, with Scenario 4 (that of 'sea of conflict' with its unknown consequences) as one most to be avoided. Although some policymakers - whether in China, Southeast Asia or the US – may ultimately favour stable cohabitation (Scenario 1) or regional hegemony (Scenario 2), they will generally recognise that these scenarios involve winners and potential losers. They also require the most ambitious of diplomacies, with the highest stakes. By concentrating on more modest, and arguably more achievable, ambitions – that of managing mistrust – all powers can protect their stake in the ongoing evolution of the regional order. They do so too with the hope, and indeed aim, that a more low-key, incremental approach can deliver stability in the short term which, in time, can stretch into the medium term, and that this stability is, in turn, broadly inclusive of all regional interests.

Yet even such an apparently modest ambition will require greater policy engagement on the part of all protagonists in order to insure against the advent of Scenario 4 and the 'sea of conflict'. To this end, four key areas for policy engagement should be considered:

## Clarification

All parties should be urged to clarify their claims under UNCLOS. This instils a mutual recognition and reassurance of a respect for international law that would be inherently stabilising. China's nine-dashed line is not the only clarification required, but it is the most significant given its size and the fact that it has little basis in international law. Instead of fearing that its territorial and maritime claims or negotiating strategies could be undermined by any clarification, China's leadership should recognise that its interests would instead be served. Firstly, such a move would undercut a key hostile narrative of Chinese objectives to rewrite the international order. Secondly, it would shore up confidence in Chinese intentions within Southeast Asia, including its ongoing commitment to 'peaceful development', which inevitably entails the harnessing of its ever more apparent military capabilities. Importantly, such a clarification would not necessarily involve the acceptance of third-party arbitration facilities offered under the Law of the Sea; parties would continue to be legally entitled to reject such an option.[12] Meanwhile, China's clarification of its island claims in the East China Sea should spur those lobbying for reciprocal consistency in the South China Sea, censuring China on its apparent preference for strategic ambiguity as a deliberate negotiating tactic.

It should be noted that the responsibilities of clarification are not China's alone. Although Vietnam has stated that it claims all of the Paracel and Spratly Islands, it has not clarified which islands actually qualify as lying within the Spratly grouping – does this, for example, include James Shoal lying just 100km off Malaysia's coast? The provision by all disputants of a list of maritime features would go a long way towards a basis for negotiation in the future.

Claimant parties should also consider working together to agree, at least in theory, what features carry what maritime entitlements, regardless of whose claims to sovereignty are ultimately recognised. At present, there is little informed appreciation for what maritime rights are actually at stake in the South China Sea since there is no agreed narrative on what features actually qualify as islands under UNCLOS 121(1). In turn it is unclear which of those islands are capable of sustaining human habitation or an economic life of their own, thereby generating under UNCLOS 121(3) not simply a 12nm territorial sea but also a strategically more significant EEZ or continental shelf. There has, then, been a distinct paucity of mapping what different interpretations could actually signify in terms of maritime zones and entitlements. For example, it is possible that the smaller Spratly Islands, in particular, in fact contain no features entitled to anything more than a 12 nautical mile territorial sea, especially if the definition for a capacity to sustain economic life is based on natural features rather than a state's more cynical investment in creating infrastructure on any given feature.[13]

Realistically, this work should start in areas where disputes are at least recognised and involve working groups engaging representatives of all claimants. Agreements would need to be made on all features by all sides, regardless of present occupation. And since very few of these features are actually occupied, for once there would be at least some incentive not to take the maximalist position for fear of a claim not being recognised at some future point. A working group for the Spratlys would therefore include the six claimants, although the involvement of Taiwan here would have to be negotiated.[14] A working group for Scarborough Reef, to take another example, would include only representatives from the Philippines, China and (again, subject to negotiation) Taiwan. A supervisory panel to which all the respective working groups reported could involve broader representation, for example from ASEAN or even the US. This way China's interest in bilateralism would be met, yet within a context of multilateral oversight. Mistrust would be managed through the objective assessment of maritime rights separated from questions of territorial ownership.

## Collaboration

The disputes should be carefully unpacked into their constituent parts. Disputes over territorial sovereignty are by their nature zero-sum, whereas disputes over maritime zones and freedom of navigation within EEZs need not be. More collaborative approaches to these issues could and should therefore be considered. Especially if work upon island clarification, as defined under UNCLOS, established that maritime claims within this sea were more confined than commonly believed (even allowing for claims extending from continental shelf coastlines), there should be clear established areas for potential joint development, whether in terms of hydrocarbon exploration, or protection of fishing stocks and the maritime environment.[15] Previous joint exploration agreements, between China, the Philippines and Vietnam in 2005 and between China and Japan in 2008, could still act as precedents and models for such agreements, despite their limited success historically and with lessons duly learnt.

In place of unilateral imposition of fishing bans aimed at preserving precious fish stocks, bilateral or even multilateral fishing bans should be discussed.[16] This would prevent the resentment that can occur in response to China's fishing ban and create a sense of cooperation. A moratorium on deep-sea drilling in clearly disputed areas could also be considered, with the intention to restart such drilling once clarification of island claims and respective EEZs had occurred and/or joint exploitation agreements could be reached. Perhaps less ambitiously, governments could consider the establishment of fishing hotlines to facilitate a depoliticised transfer of fishermen detained for fishing in a contested area.

A multilateral fishing ban could theoretically lead, in time, to joint or coordinated maritime paramilitary patrols across areas claimed by the parties involved. This would help increase coordination and maritime domain awareness, for example by requiring parties to acknowledge the position of any vessels, or pool resources. It should therefore minimise the possibility of confrontations (with the additional benefit of lowering the costs of patrols). There is even a precedent in China's pursuit of coordinated maritime patrols with three ASEAN states in the Mekong River (Laos, Thailand and Myanmar), which came about at Beijing's request following the murder of 13 Chinese citizens in October 2011.

Obviously, the South China Sea presents a more complicated set of problems, not least of which is the fact that maritime paramilitary patrols are, in reality, designed to accomplish a number of tasks, only one of which is fishery regulation. In as much as they also fulfil the role of demonstrating de facto sovereignty over the area, these are missions individual countries are unlikely to wish to forgo in the short term. Nonetheless, there are a variety of other tasks that could be accomplished by regional states' paramilitary forces which would also encourage greater collaboration. The May 2011 Arctic Council's search-and-rescue (SAR) agreement is one example of an accord between countries with often fractious relations and existing maritime disputes, which was designed to delineate and outline cooperation in a particular maritime role. For similar reasons, SAR could be a mission that could be jointly or cooperatively accomplished in the South China Sea, allowing littoral states to harmonise their paramilitary operations and thus minimise the opportunities for potential altercations.

Finally, and already under discussion, is a form of 'incidents at sea' agreement (INCSEA). This would be informed by the experiences of the 1972 agreement between the US and the USSR, but modelled according to today's particular circumstances and regional requirements. Such an agreement would be a substantive contribution towards helping mitigate the risk of escalatory conflict (Scenario 4) and would, in and of itself, build confidence towards the more favourable outcome of managed mistrust (Scenario 3). Currently promoted by the US and regarded with suspicion by China, Southeast Asian nations have an important role to play in pushing for the development of such a safety valve in their own waters. An ancillary benefit of INCSEA agreements is that they formalise military–military contacts through annual workshops that discuss matters at hand, something currently pursued in Sino-US relations but without the inclusive involvement of Southeast Asian nations.

## Contextualisation

The tensions which underpin disputes in the South China Sea should continue to be tackled in their own right rather than being allowed to fester within this already complex picture of regional relations. As this book has argued, rapidly expanding Chinese military capabilities are fuelling regional mistrust. Although China's right to spend its growing resources on an increased military capability is not contested, the reality is that the often deliberate opaqueness to these advancements is further fuelling the inevitable anxieties these developments are causing, both amongst the smaller and medium-sized powers of the region, as well as on the part of the established regional hegemon, the US. Regular, high-level dialogues between militaries and their governments therefore become all the more important in explaining intentions and minimising the room for misunderstanding and miscalculation.

Yet even with greater transparency, US interests in the additional reassurances provided by a continued surveillance of China's rise would realistically remain. In other words, disputes over freedom of passage for military vessels in an EEZ are a stand-alone factor fuelling tensions in the South China Sea, even if they are tied into China's military advancements. Here, the US would be well served to argue both internationally and bilaterally. Internationally, it has to continue to seek to engage other countries which benefit either directly, or indirectly, from US security patronage in support of its argument on EEZ interpretations. It should also highlight the dangers inherent in accepting distinctions between commercial and military rights of passage. After all, in particular with the blurring of lines over paramilitaries and the engagement of militaries in humanitarian disasters and contingency planning, who is the ultimate arbiter of what vessel is or is not 'civilian' or 'for peaceful purposes'? Bilaterally, the US can discuss with China its own pragmatic interests in the protection of such capabilities against the day in which Chinese vessels might wish to conduct similar activities against other nations – and, arguably, this already occurs in disputed waters in the South China Sea and Pacific Ocean. Ultimately, knowledge and transparency are empowering – they build confidence and therefore add to stability rather than undermine it. The better the strategic picture is understood, the less likely a miscalculation, and with it a possible descent into conflict.

More broadly, US, Chinese and Southeast Asian interests would all be served by a contextualisation of South China Sea's disputes outside of the framework of a rising China and the reactions of the US as the established hegemon. Instead these disputes can be placed within a broader context of discussions on international law, as well as the evolving regional order in Southeast Asia, thereby including other partners from beyond the immediate region – from South Asia, East Asia and Australasia, for example. The alternative, an exaggerated focus on the US–China backdrop and the story of great-power dynamics, risks turning a situation which does not have to be zero-sum into one more likely to be perceived as such. Once more, Southeast Asian states have a critical role to play in this rejection of a narrower, and potentially inflammatory, focus, in favour of this broader contextualisation.

## Civilianisation

Once again this is an issue of framing as much as content. The aim should be to 'de-securitise' the disputes, protecting them as a topic of civilian control and concern, with military influences and involvement kept to a minimum. Militaries are, by their design, devised to detect threats and deal with them. They think the worst of each other, and prepare for the worst. So-called 'hardliners' are therefore understandably to be found more in military than in civilian worlds, although of course countervailing voices can be found in both.

In the protection of established sovereignty the military, naturally, has a key role to play. Yet in the management of disputed territory, the danger is that the military becomes part of the policymaking process, rather than a servant of it. Some dynamic to this effect can already be seen in the internal competitions for budgets between government agencies. This is particularly the case in China where the military has long been a key bastion of influence on security-related issues (for example, relations with the DPRK). And so, whilst military–military dialogues are important for maintaining lines of communication and handling incidents at sea, discussion of the management of claims in the South China Sea should be framed, where possible, by civilian actors in civilian terms. The apparent use, for example, of retired PLA officers to issue hardline articles on Chinese entitlements in the South China Sea either by way of venting nationalist sentiment or by way of a test balloon for future actions, runs directly against this, and in the process, further militarises an already strained environment. Meanwhile, an already disempowered MFA is left to conduct damage control. Although the impetus would have to come bilaterally, even the briefest of regular multilateral meetings between claimant MFAs could send an important symbolic indication to the region and beyond about the determination of actors to contain tensions within the civilian arena, avoiding their escalation to necessarily more hardline, military rhetoric. Regularity could be key to the success of such an initiative, as an annual meeting of MFAs dedicated to discussion of security in the South China Sea would demonstrate the central role being played by the civilian ministries, rather than the defence ministries, in management of these disputes. It would also provide a channel of communication on relevant issues. Such meetings would not necessarily be framed around conflict resolution, thus avoiding China's concerns over multilateral solutions to the disagreements, but simply information exchange, for example, on actions in counter-piracy or marine environment protection.

Within this context of 'civilianisation', other more dramatic measures could be considered. Realistically, under the incremental approach being proposed, these more ambitious measures would only be appropriate in time, but could, for example, extend to a freeze on the upgrading of any military infrastructure on islands already occupied. The DoC asks signatories to engage in 'self-restraint' with regard to developments, but the only example of this cited is the requirement to refrain from the militarisation of further features. Indeed, its relative success in limiting *new* occupations since 2002 might suggest that a similar agreement could prove feasible in restricting the further expansion of current occupations. Such a freeze could be achievable in that it would effectively cement Chinese (and Vietnamese) military superiority on key structures, but in return for the guarantee that further divergences in finance and capabilities between claimants would not be deployed to fuel the existing disparities in military presence.[17] The longer-term goal of such an agreement would be the civilianisation of these occupations: transferring responsibility for the management of the features from the military to paramilitary agencies. Indeed,

Taiwan has already attempted to pursue this demilitarisation tactic, replacing its marines for Coast Guard Administration officials in 2000 on Itu Aba. Given the rising importance of maritime paramilitary agencies in the region generally, this would seem a logical step that could have the benefit of further distancing the military from the equation, minimising the likelihood of any repeat of the bloody military clashes of 1974 and 1988.

## The South China Sea and the regional order

The South China Sea is rightly capturing the attention of policymakers both within and beyond the immediate region. Tensions there have potentially global implications, both with regard to their interim management as well as their ultimate resolution. Alongside the potential consequences of poorly managed disputes over territorial sovereignty and maritime zones for stability in the region lies the more theoretical, but definitively global implications, for the rule of international law in general, and the interpretation of the Law of the Sea in particular. Meanwhile *how* China in particular chooses to deploy its growing naval might in the South China Sea will offer broader clues as to its prospects for a continued peaceful rise.

Much as it might occasionally suit US interests to frame the debate otherwise, the broader issue at stake in the South China Sea is not about the danger of a deliberate assault on freedom of navigation per se.[18] As a major trading nation itself, and one whose stability is peculiarly linked to its thriving economy, China has little interest in tactics that would seriously threaten sea lines of communication. Instead, the broader issue is the struggle to influence how the regional order develops, both in terms of hard-power postures in the region, and in more theoretical terms with regard to the values and norms espoused by an emerging regional order.

The management of tensions in the South China Sea will therefore help determine whether the narrative of this regional order is one of cooperation – with the positive spin-off effects this could bring for great-power relations more generally – or one of competition, or even conflict. The story of the South China Sea disputes is, then, one of US, Chinese and Southeast Asian efforts to manage the impact of China's rise in an emerging region where the balance of power is still being decided. It is the story of the intersection of great-power politics with the interests of small and medium-sized powers. In other words, the story of the South China Sea is something of a microcosm for the story of Asia-Pacific security in the twenty-first century.

## Notes

[1] This is a scenario advocated beyond China, including by Hugh White, who makes specific reference to the danger of escalatory conflict in the South China Sea. Hugh White, *The China Choice* (Collingwood: Black Inc., 2012).

[2] Interview with Paul Keating, *ABC*, 23 Nov 2011. Transcript available at: http://www.abc.net.au/lateline/content/2011/s3374642.htm.

[3] To some extent, the US 'pivot' has instituted this policy, rebalancing US forces away from China's immediate neighbourhood, even while maintaining a bolstered rhetorical and physical defence posture in the region more broadly.

[4] James Holmes, 'Rough Waters for Coalition Building', in Cronin (ed.), *Cooperation from Strength*, p. 107.

[5] This tributary system reached its zenith under the Ming dynasty (1368–1644), following considerable expansion in the wake of China's great maritime expeditions of the early 1400s.

[6] For more on this argument, see, for example: James Dobbins, 'War with China'.

[7] The US has argued that this Mutual Defence Treaty does not apply to Scarborough Reef since the formal registration of Philippine claims here postdate the signing of this treaty. However, this is a somewhat technical argument. Were the Philippines to be the clear victims of Chinese aggression and the US fail to intervene in support of its ally in the region, regional perceptions of the advantages that come from a close alignment with the US would be severely damaged, with a consequent negative impact on the US's standing within the emerging regional order the likely result.

8  See: Fravel, *Strong Borders, Secure Nation*, chapter 4.

9  This was the label attached by Cronin and Kaplan to the US strategy of maintaining naval primacy within a broader framework of regional cooperation. Cronin and Kaplan, 'Cooperation from Strength', p. 5.

10  The US has, in the past, also used mil–mil relations to make broader political points. For example, they were the ones who shut down cooperation in the wake of the EP-3 incident in 2001.

11  This point is well made by Cronin and Kaplan as they dismiss any temptation to over-emphasise the influence of either a more authoritarian or a more democratic China on the South China Sea. Cronin and Kaplan, 'Cooperation from Strength', p. 15.

12  China is far from the only state which has explicitly rejected this option. Similarly, the US would likely reject such an option were it ever to ratify UNCLOS.

13  For more on this argument, see: Tonnesson, 'China's Changing Role in the South China Sea', *Asia Quarterly*, vol. 12, no. 3 & 4, Winter 2012, pp. 18–30.

14  China should be amenable to Taiwanese inclusion in that their overlapping claims effectively give China two seats at the table, rather than one (or none in the case of Taiwan).

15  This has similarities with the Philippine proposal for a Zone of Peace, Freedom, Friendship and Cooperation (ZoPFFC), as referenced in chapter 3.

16  This could only be countenanced in areas where claims overlapped in such a way that both claimants would have to compromise in allowing the other paramilitary on to their claimed territory. The JMSU collapsed as a confidence-building measure in part because of Philippine objections that its mandate only involved exploration in an area claimed by the Philippines, with no apparent reciprocal gesture made on the part of China or Vietnam.

17  Negotiations would have to be carefully managed to avoid a flurry of militarisation shortly before any such agreement.

18  The authors do accept, however, aside from questions over access by military vessels, an important distinction in emphasis on the question of EEZs. Under international law, EEZs are presented as international waters in which the adjacent country has particular rights. China's approach appears to suggest it views EEZs as the adjacent country's waters in which other countries have particular rights, premised on host-country agreement.

# The legal environment in the South China Sea

According to the 2002 Declaration on the Conduct of Parties in the South China Sea, all the signatories have undertaken to resolve their disagreements over the various disputes by peaceful means, 'in accordance with universally recognised principles of international law, including the 1982 UN Convention on the Law of the Sea.' All of the claimants in the South China Sea bar Taiwan have signed the DoC and have ratified UNCLOS. (Taiwan, which is not recognised as a state under Article 306 of UNCLOS, is thereby prevented from signing the convention).[1]

What does this actually mean for the management of these disputes? UNCLOS is a broad international agreement that emanated from the third UN Conference on the Law of the Sea between 1973 and 1982, with the resultant convention finally coming into force in 1994. The same year an additional agreement was adopted to implement the provisions of Part XI of UNCLOS relating to the resources of the deep seabed outside the limits of any nation's jurisdiction.

It remains the foremost international legal instrument dedicated to maritime affairs, acting as a sort of constitution for the oceans.

Containing 320 articles in its main body and a further 116 in its nine annexes, UNCLOS is a weighty document that covers key areas such as maritime jurisdiction, rights, responsibilities, science, technology, resources and environmental preservation. At its heart is a division of the sea and sub-sea area into zones that delimitate a particular state's sovereignty and rights of usage.

In effect, each state has a set of concentric areas in its adjacent waters that decrease in levels of sovereignty and rights as they extend outwards from the shoreline. The closest zone to any state's shoreline (beyond its internal waters or archipelagic waters) is the territorial sea – a 12nm band measured from the low-water line of the shore or agreed baselines in which the airspace, water column, seabed and sub-soil area is the sovereign territory of the state. Where the territorial seas of two or more states overlap, a median line will delimit them.

While the state has sovereignty over its territorial zone, exclusive rights to all resources within it and can regulate the activity of vessels in areas including safety, conservation, traffic and customs, it does not have total dominion over every transiting ship. As Article 17 states, 'all ships enjoy the right of innocent passage through the territorial sea,' and should therefore be able to transit without interference, assuming they are acting legally. Even warships enjoy the right of innocent passage within a coastal state's territorial sea, although submarines are required to surface and show the flag.

Beyond the territorial sea, the EEZ extends out to 200nm from the baselines. The first 12nm of this area beyond the territorial sea (hence, from 12nm to 24nm) is the contiguous zone. The state does not have sovereignty over this area, but has the ability to prevent and punish infringement of its customs, fiscal, immigration and sanitary laws. In line with the rest of the EEZ, the state also enjoys 'sovereign rights' over the exploration, exploitation, conservation and management of natural resources in the water, seabed and subsoil in this area. Outside of the contiguous zone and the specific regulation of natural resources, the EEZ is otherwise perceived to be analogous to the high seas (the area beyond all EEZs) in that all states have, for example, the right of freedom of navigation, overflight, fishing and scientific research. Finally, there is the possibility that a coastal state may have rights to the resources in the seabed and subsoil beyond the EEZ should it be proven that its continental shelf extends beyond the 200nm EEZ. The maximum extent of this extended continental shelf is 350nm from the state's baselines.

This delineation of areas of responsibility appears clearly to outline the rights and responsibilities of each state. However, with regard to the South China Sea there are several difficulties that arise from the implementation of UNCLOS.

## The limits of the convention

UNCLOS is an attempt to codify the legal environment on the seas; it does not seek to define the manner in which disputes to sovereignty over land, including offshore islands, can be resolved. This is important because despite the expansive Sino-Taiwanese nine-dashed line over the 'historical waters' of the South China Sea, the disputes are in essence disagreements over the sovereignty of land – namely, the various islands and features in the sea. UNCLOS's direct role in the settlement of sovereignty disputes over the islands of the South China Sea is therefore necessarily limited. (Nevertheless, UNCLOS is of key relevance to the South China Sea with regard to its provisions on issues such as baselines, EEZs, continental shelves, maritime boundary delimitation, and distinctions between rocks, low-tide elevations and islands – all areas where there are evident and ongoing disputes between claimants.)

With regard to sea claims, whilst UNCLOS encourages its state parties to reach agreement on any disputes through negotiation, if this proves impossible, four compulsory and binding options for arbitration are presented:

i. the International Tribunal for the Law of the Sea (ITLOS) in Hamburg, Germany;

ii. the International Court of Justice in The Hague, The Netherlands;

iii. a 'special arbitral tribunal' constituted for certain categories of disputes (established under Annex VIII of UNCLOS);

iv. ad hoc arbitration (in accordance with Annex VII of UNCLOS). This is the default means of dispute resolution where no preference has been expressed by a given state.[2]

Under Article 287(1), states are offered the opportunity to make declarations on which of these forums for dispute resolution are acceptable to the particular state. Where states have opted for different dispute-resolution procedures, under Article 287(5), arbitration takes place under Annex VII, in other words on an ad hoc basis. Since none of the claimants have made an election under Article 287, if the compulsory binding dispute-settlement mechanism were to be invoked in the sea, the claims would go for ad hoc arbitration under Annex VII.

Importantly, however, Section 3 of Part V of UNCLOS also allows states to opt out, at any time, of all compulsory binding arbitration procedures with regard to certain specified categories of disputes. This includes (under Article 298) certain sea boundary delimitation disputes, as well as disputes over 'military activities' and 'law enforcement activities with regard to the exercise of sovereign rights'.[3]

The individual positions of the claimant states with regard to these Articles are, then, important in defining the prospects for independent dispute resolution under international law. At the time of its ratification in 1996, China, for example, made a statement affirming 'its sovereignty over all its archipelagos and islands as listed in article 2 of the Law of the People's Republic of China on the territorial sea and the contiguous zone, which was promulgated on 25 February 1992'. Interestingly, with regard to its parallel tussle with the US over military surveillance activities within its EEZ, the same statement also noted China's position that the law providing for 'innocent passage' did not 'prejudice the right of a coastal State to request … a foreign State to obtain advance approval from or give prior notification to the coastal State for the passage of its warships through the territorial sea of the coastal State.' Perhaps more importantly though, in 2006, China followed up this statement with a declaration under Article 298 which simply noted: 'The Government of the People's Republic of China does not accept any of the procedures provided for in Section 2 of Part XV of the Convention with respect to all the categories of disputes referred to in paragraph 1 (a) (b) and (c) of Article 298 of the Convention.'[4] It remains the only one of the claimant states to have exercised its right to such an opt-out. In practical terms, this renders the prospects for external dispute-arbitration moot. The attempt by the Philippines in January 2013 to submit its competing claims with China in the South China Sea to an arbitral tribunal is thus likely to be stymied.[5] While the process of the tribunal referral may yet have diplomatic benefits for the Philippines and even perhaps encourage greater clarification on the details of claims, this legal path is unlikely to bring resolution in and of its self.

Other claimants have likewise taken the opportunity of ratification to make statements reaffirming their sovereignty claims in the South China Sea, noting that their signature not be allowed to prejudice their position there. Vietnam made a statement upon ratification (in 1994) reiterating its sovereignty 'over the Hoang Sa and Truong Sa archipelagos', authorising the Vietnamese government to 'undertake effective measures for the management and defence of the continental shelf and maritime zones of Viet Nam'.[6] Similarly, the Philippines deposited a statement upon ratification (in 1984) noting the agreement did not 'impair or prejudice the sovereignty of the Republic of the Philippines over any territory over which it exercises sovereign authority'. It referenced Article 298 only to note that any submission to dispute resolution under the Convention 'not be considered a derogation of Philippines sovereignty'.[7] Upon its ratification (in 1996), Malaysia likewise noted that its ratification 'in no way constitutes recognition of the maritime claims of any other State … where such claims are … prejudicial to the sovereign rights and jurisdiction of Malaysia in its maritime areas'. In a position closer to that of China, it also specifically referenced the passage of military vessels, noting its interpretation that 'the provisions of the Convention do not authorize other States to carry out military exercises or manoeuvres … in the exclusive economic zone without the consent of the coastal State'.[8] However, not only has Malaysia not opted out under Article 298, in 2003 it took a dispute over land reclamation with its neighbour Singapore to an ad hoc dispute resolution under Annex VII of UNCLOS by the Permanent Court of Arbitration, abiding by the eventual award made by the tribunal in 2005.[9] Lastly, Brunei ratified UNCLOS in 1996 but deposited no statement and has exercised no opt out under Article 298.

## The tensions of its interpretation

Certain statements within the convention continue to be interpreted by signatory states in different ways, bringing associated tensions. For example, when outlining the responsibilities of states other than the coastal state in an EEZ, Article 58 mentions that 'states shall have due regard to the rights and duties of the coastal state and shall comply with the laws and regulations adopted by the coastal state in accordance with the provisions of this convention'. As indicated above, some states have interpreted this article, bolstered by customary international law, to indicate that any military activity by another state should be preceded by a request to the coastal state.

Similarly, of particular relevance to the South China Sea disputes is Article 121 of UNCLOS, which defines what is and is not an island. In just three short sub-articles, the convention states that an island must be naturally formed and above water at high tide. This is easily measured, but it also differentiates between islands that may claim a 200nm EEZ and 'rocks', which are incapable of sustaining 'human habitation or economic life of their own', which have no EEZ and may only claim a 12nm territorial sea. The difference between the two is substantial: tens of thousands of miles of EEZ depend on whether a feature is defined as an island or as a rock. Thus, there is a great incentive for states to try to prove the ability of a promontory to sustain human habitation. There is also an incentive for states to claim that their occupations on fortified reefs and shoals are natural islands rather than artificial constructions on submerged features. As this book has argued, the failure thus far to define which features are islands and which are rocks is a key aspect of the continuing disputes in the South China Sea.

## The US and UNCLOS

Whilst UNCLOS has been ratified by more than 165 other states, the US has signed the treaty but never ratified it. Indeed, when UNCLOS was first negotiated, then President Ronald Reagan objected to the treaty as prejudicial to the economic and security interests of the US. This was, in particular, due to Part XI of the Convention which established a regime relating to mineral extraction in the seabed beyond any state's EEZ and an International Seabed Authority (ISA) to authorise the exploration and mining of such minerals, including the collection and distribution of mining royalties. A major revision in 1994 was agreed precisely to address the concerns of the US in this regard; the US, then under President Bill Clinton, duly acceded to the treaty.[10] Yet its ratification has proved a consistent and elusive challenge for subsequent administrations, including most recently President Barack Obama following his abortive attempt in 2012 to secure the two-thirds majority in the US Senate required to ratify the treaty. This despite vocal support from Secretary of State Hillary Clinton, Defense Secretary Leon Panetta and Chairman of the Joint Chiefs of Staff General Martin Dempsey.

The absence of the US from those that have ratified the treaty appears odd when one considers that it was a key force behind the creation of the initial convention, as well as its subsequent revision in 1994, negotiating many provisions to its advantage in the process. Indeed, with nearly 12,500 miles of coastline, 360 major commercial ports and the world's largest exclusive economic zone, not to mention the diplomatic and military arguments for ratification, there should be strong commercial logic for full US support for the most significant legal framework in existence for the management of international waters.[11]

Yet it is important to note that the US has been consistently clear that it recognises UNCLOS as customary international law, and to that end it has respected and promulgated all the provisions of UNCLOS since 1994. This arguably makes its non-ratification more of a diplomatic issue than a legal one. Ultimately, it may appear hypocritical to some for the US to be lecturing others on the importance of respecting the provisions of a treaty it has repeatedly failed to ratify, but the reality remains that the US has been a fervent respecter and upholder of the provisions of UNCLOS, including with regard to territorial delimitation and the rights of vessels and persons within these zones. Indeed, one reason that the US military leadership have long been understood to be strongly supportive of the treaty is, in part, because it is understood to secure US rights over its territorial waters. Whilst US calls for all claimants to respect UNCLOS as the key framework for dispute management in the South China Sea (and the suggestion that China in particular help by clarifying its claims here under UNCLOS) can therefore be presented as problematic, the reality is that US behaviour in this international arena has been consistent and clear.

## Conclusion

Sadly, UNCLOS is unlikely to be the legal panacea to dispute resolution in the South China Sea that some hope. It is a comprehensive and useful convention for clarifying what states are legally able to claim, but without clarification from all the claimants as to the precise nature of their claims and with opt outs on dispute resolution exercised, there is little in the convention that suggests it can singlehandedly provide the answer for dispute resolution in the South China Sea. Even without the shortcomings of UNCLOS' reach and the questions over its interpretation, there are, as this book has argued, other important geopolitical and geoeconomic factors in play that will also prove important influences in informing the nature and handling of this particular set of sovereignty disputes.

It is nevertheless encouraging to note that, in particular, since the 2009 deadline for notification of state claims to an extended continental shelf, all of the ASEAN claimants have taken – to greater or lesser extent – important steps towards bringing their claims into line with UNCLOS, accepting that claims to natural resources at sea can only be derived from claims to land features. Even Taiwan, unable to sign up to UNCLOS officially, has taken steps to bring its domestic legislation on its claims in the sea into line with UNCLOS.[12] China remains the outlier here, yet to clarify both the extent and the basis of its claims – whether they are based on claims to land features in accordance with UNCLOS or whether it is claiming rights in the entirety of the maritime area within its nine-dashed line.

In the long term, the ratification of UNCLOS by all disputants should provide a basic framework under which each state outlines its specific claim, whilst also providing an important aid in negotiation and dispute management. However, in the short term, the passage of UNCLOS with its associated demands on its signatories has arguably exacerbated competition between the littoral states, not least by outlining exactly how much of the South China Sea and its natural resources are at stake.

## Notes

1  See: Status of UNCLOS, UN Treaty Collection Database, http://treaties. un.org/pages/ViewDetailsIII. aspx?&src=TREATY&mtdsg_no=X XI~6&chapter=21&Temp=mtdsg3&l ang=en.

2  For further details on this, see the explanation of UNCLOS arbitration procedures offered by the Permanent Court of Arbitration in the Hague: http://www.pca-cpa. org/showpage.asp?pag_id=1288.

3  For more information on declarations made under Article 298 see the website of United Nations Division for Ocean Affairs and the Law of the Sea: http://www.un.org/ Depts/los/convention_agreements/ convention_declarations.htm.

4  Ibid.

5  The case being brought by the Philippines is fairly wide ranging, including requests for China's nine-dashed line to be declared invalid under UNCLOS, and claiming that Chinese-occupied Mischief and McKennan Reef are submerged features that form part of the continental shelf of the Philippines, and that Chinese-occupied Gaven and Subi Reef are submerged features rather than islands. For further details of the Philippines's 'Notification and Statement of Claim', see: 'Philippines Submits South China Sea Disputes with China to UNCLOS Annex VII Arbitration', International

Boundaries Research Unit, Durham University, 22 January 2013. https://www.dur.ac.uk/ibru/news/ boundary_news/?itemno=16498.

6 For details on declarations made, see: http://www.un.org/Depts/ los/convention_agreements/ convention_declarations.htm.

7 *Ibid.*

8 *Ibid.*

9 For details of this referral and award, see: http://www.pca-cpa. org/showpage.asp?pag_id=1154.

10 For a more extensive analysis of how the 1994 agreement on implementation sought to address Reagan's concerns with regard to the deep seabed mining provisions contained in UNCLOS, see: Bernard Oxman,'The 1994 Agreement and the Convention', *The American Journal of International Law*, vol. 88, 1994, pp. 687–96.

11 Thad W. Allen, Richard L. Armitage and John J. Hamre, 'Odd Man Out at Sea: The US and UNCLOS', CSIS Asia Policy Blog, 25 April 2012.

12 See, for example: Song Yann-Huei and Keyuan Zou, 'Maritime Legislation of Mainland China and Taiwan: Developments, Comparison, Implications, and Potential Challenges for the United States', *Ocean Development and International Law*, vol. 31, no. 4, 2000, pp. 303–45.